D1833262

THE ROLE OF REGIONAL POLITICAL PARTIES IN INDIAN COALITION POLITICS : A CASE STUDY OF TAMIL NADU

The Role of Regional Political Parties in Indian Coalition Politics

A Case Study of Tamil Nadu

Mouneshwara Srinivasrao

KALPAZ

© **Author**

All rights reserved. No part of this book may be reproduced, stored, adapted, or transmitted in any form or by any means, electronic, mechanical, photocopying, micro-filming, recording or otherwise, or translated in any language, without the prior written permission of the copyright owner and the publisher. The book is sold subject to the condition that it shall not, by way of trade or otherwise, be lent, resold, hired out, or otherwise circulated without the prior publisher's written consent in any form of binding or cover other than that in which it is published.

The views and opinions expressed in this book are author(s) own and the facts reported by them have been verified to the extent possible, and the publishers are not in any way liable for the same.

ISBN: 978-93-5128-115-3
Price : ₹ 675

First Published, 2015

Published by

Kalpaz Publications
C-30, Satyawati Nagar,
Delhi-110052
Ph. : 9212142040
E-mail: kalpaz@hotmail.com

Laser Typesetting : Abhishek Mandal, Delhi
Printed at : G. Print Process, Delhi

Cataloging in Publication Data—DK
Courtesy: D.K. Agencies (P) Ltd. <docinfo@dkagencies.com>

Srinivasrao, Mouneshwara, author.
The role of regional political parties in Indian coalition politics : a case study of Tamil Nadu / Dr Mouneshwara Srinivasrao.
pages cm
Includes bibliographical references (pages) and index.
ISBN 9789351281153

1. Political parties—India—Tamil Nadu. 2. Regionalism—India—Tamil Nadu. 3. Coalition governments—India—Tamil Nadu. 4. Tamil Nadu (India)—Politics and government—20th century. I. Title.

DDC 324.254011095482 23

Contents

Acknowledgements

In India the coalition governments have mainly been the result of multi-party system. As sometimes, single political party was able to muster clear-cut majority in the Legislative Assembly, the parties were obliged to seek support and cooperation of other groups to form the government. Sometimes coalitions are also formed before the elections and a number of political parties chalk out an agreed programme and contest elections on the basis of the programme from a common platform. This type of arrangement has an obvious advantage in so far as it smoothens the radicalism the parties joining the coalition without in any way effecting the existing image.

The coalition politics made its beginning in a big way in the states only in the wake of the Fourth General Elections of 1967 when the Congress party, which had enjoyed monopoly of political power both at the centre as well as the states, was voted out of power in seven out of the seventeen states. Except in Tamil Nadu, where the DMK obtained a clear-cut majority, the other six states no single political party was able to obtain a clear-cut majority. This compelled the various political parties to join hands to keep the Congress Government out of power. Thus, started the experiment of coalition governments in a big way, which however did not last long. Soon partners of these coalition government fell apart and brought about the decline of coalition governments; thereby contributing to the political instability in these states.

It is clear that the working of coalition government in various states as well as the centre that the experiment lasted for a limited duration only. In most of the states coalition politics prevailed between the year 1967 and 1971 when the Congress strength in some of the state Legislative Assemblies was considerably reduced and the political parties professing faith in different ideology and programme joined hands to capture the power without bothering about a common programme. Once in power the members of the coalition fought for offices and portfolios and did not mind pulling down thc credibility of other partners in public estimation to further their own interests. Individual members as well as groups frequently indulged in horse trading and changed their loyalties. This gave rise to the evil of defection. It has been asserted that more defections took place between 1967 and 1971 than during the first fifteen years. This was so because the different political parties welcomed defectors to retain the majority, which was so essential to keep themselves in power.

I incurred many debts in this creative process to turn as a book of my research work. Like any academic effort this one too owes its form and substance to many without whom it would not have been possible for me to bring this work to completion. The limitations and inadequacies in this effort are, however, solely mine.

So many people have shared my delight in this activity that I may have to forgo referring to all the names. However, I pay my gratitude to all of them.

I owe a deep sense of gratitude to my teacher and research supervisor, **Dr S.A. Palekar,** Professor, Department of Political Science, and Dean, Faculty of Social Science, Gulbarga University, Gulbarga, for his constant guidance, encouragement and generous treatment for this work.

Similarly, my sincere thanks to my teachers **Prof. B.M. Baeen, Prof. (Smt.) Hemalatha Jayaraj, Prof. Chandranakanth Yatanoor, Prof. P.B. Rathod, Prof. Gooru Sree Ramulu,** for their valuable suggestions.

My gratitude knows no bounds, where words just fall to short to express my love to the north star of my life, my loving and affectionate parents **Sri Srinivasrao** and **Smt Eshwaramma**.

My heartful thanks are also due to my friends, Dr Krishna Namdev, Dr Ambaraya S. Hagaragi for their moral support.

I hold out my sincere thanks to Mr. Amit Garg for his committed and efficient secretarial help.

Special thanks are extended to my publisher, Kalpaz Publications, and the editorial team for their efforts in bringing out the book.

Dr Mouneshwara Srinivasrao

Foreword

In the federal-parliamentary democracy consists of an elected representative Parliament which is supreme, a Cabinet collectively responsible to Parliament, a Prime Minister who is supreme within the Cabinet and an organised opposition within the Parliament. It was assumed that the majority would form the government and the minority would function as the opposition. Problems arose when no party could secure enough majority to form a single-party government, and in such circumstances the alternative was the coalition or multi-party government. This situation invariably leads to some changes in the traditional paradigm of parliamentary democracy. The composition of Cabinet, the nature of its working, the style of the Prime Minister/Chief Minister, the character of electoral politics and the party system, and even the composition of the legislature to a limited extent are likely to be affected by the nature of coalition politics. Although the UK had brief spells of coalition governments, they did not last long enough to change the institutional character. It is left to other countries that are compelled to work continuous coalitions to modify the parliamentary institutions.

Coalition building between two or more parties has been frequent in Europe. Between 1990 and 1995 there were no less than 91 Cabinets in office, of which 19 were single-party governments, 69 multi-party governments and four caretaker governments. Nevertheless they have not institutionalised coalition politics apart from the parliamentary system. Switzerland is the only exception in Europe with a permanent coalition government by means of its seven-member Federal Council, elected for a fixed four-year term by the Federal Assembly on a party proportional basis. Once the election results are known in Switzerland, it is a question of simple arithmetic as to how the Cabinet seats will be distributed among the parties. The process of Cabinet formation here does not create clear winners and losers. As a result stability is very high in the Swiss case, especially since there exists no vote of non-confidence.

The present volume admirably addresses these issues which are of considerable contemporary relevance. As we seen the emergence of regional political parties because the regional political leaders wanted to assert their importance and the feeling of regionalism has been very strong in India and has manifested itself in the shape of demand for separated state, inter-state disputes and sometimes even succession from the union. The regional feelings of regionalism in India have been partly due to feelings of neglect and discrimination among certain areas or sections and partly due to the growing political awareness of the henceforth-backward people.

India has had the experience of coalition governments in the State as well as the Centre in recent times. As author analyses the coalitions in India he has to keep in mind the background of various experiments of coalitions of different parts of the world.

The present volume is going to be of great topical value to the students of Political Science, researchers, readers as well as Indian politicians. I congratulate the author to publish his research work as in book form.

Prof. S.A. Palekar

1

Introduction

The Indian political system is developing and dynamic system. It has been regularly undergoing important political and constitutional changes. Its party system too has been changing in accordance with the changes in the socio-economic environment. The transformation of several political parties from apposition of strength to weakness and vice-versa has been taking place. The Congress, which dominated the Indian political scene in the past, has suffered a decline and splinterisations. It has been the source of the birth of several small political parties in India. Because India has already emphasised multi-party system it marked not only by the presence of national political parties but also by the presence of large number of regional political parties.

Regional political parties emerged because the regional political leaders wanted to assert their importance and the feeling of regionalism has been very strong in India and has manifested itself in the shape of demand for separate state, inter-state disputes and sometimes even succession from the union. The regional feelings of regionalism in India have been partly due to feelings of neglect and discrimination among certain areas or sections and partly due to the growing political awareness of the henceforth-backward people.

India has had the experience of coalition governments in the State as well as the Centre in recent times. As we analyse the coalitions in India we have to keep in mind the background of various experiments of coalitions of different parts of the world.

There was, however, a gradual shift from the pattern of one dominant party rule. The growing political, social, economic and regional tensions gave rise to the emergence of different parties which wielded varying influences in states. In course of time an uneven political pattern was evolved. In those States where non-Congress parties mustered enough combined strength to have the working majority in State legislatures, coalition governments were formed in number of states. The year 1967 turned out to be a watershed in Indian politics, on the crest of mounting non-Congressism, non-Congress coalition governments were formed in several states. They had ideological heterogeneity. The exceptions were coalitions in West Bengal and Kerala. The coalition in West Bengal was an alliance of Left parties whereas in Kerala there was a coalition government of Left and Democratic Front.

Generally, the coalitions are found when no single political party is able to secure a working majority in the popular house on account of the presence of multi-party system. Under these circumstances a number of like-minded political parties from the coalition to provide a workable majority and run the government. France provides a typical example of this type of coalition. A coalition may be necessitated by a national crisis when the various political groups may suspend their political strife and collaborate in the general cause of protecting and promoting their national interests. In Britain, coalition government was formed to deal with the abnormal conditions during the First World War. The various political parties sunk their differences to give a united fight to the enemies of Britain.

In India, the coalition governments have mainly been the result of multi-party system. As sometimes so single political party was able to muster clear-cut majority in the Legislative Assembly the parties were obliged to seek support and cooperation of other groups to form the government. Sometimes coalitions are also formed before the elections and a number of political parties chalk out an agreed programme and contest elections on the basis of the programme from a common platform.[1] This type of arrangement has an obvious advantage in so far as it smoothens the radicalism the parties joining the coalition without in any way effecting the existing image.

The coalition politics in the states made its beginning in a big way in the states only in the wake of the Fourth General Elections of 1967 when the Congress party, which had enjoyed monopoly of political power both at the centre as well as the states, was voted out of power in seven out of the seventeen states. Except in Tamil Nadu, where the DMK obtained a clear-cut majority, the other six states no single political party was able to obtain a clear-cut majority. This compelled the various political parties to join hands to keep the Congress government out of power. Thus, started the experiment of coalition governments in a big way, which however did not last long. Soon partners of these coalition government fell apart and brought about the decline of coalition governments; thereby contributing to the political instability in these states.

It is clear that the working of coalition government in various states as well as the centre that the experiment lasted for a limited duration only. In most of the states coalition politics prevailed between the year 1967 and 1971 when the Congress strength in some of the state Legislative Assemblies was considerably reduced and the political parties professing faith in different ideology and programme joined hands to capture the power without bothering about a common programme. Once in power the members of the coalition fought for offices and portfolios and did not mind pulling down the credibility of other partners in public estimation to further their own interests. Individual members as well as groups frequently indulged in horse trading and changed their loyalties. This gave rise to the evil of defection. It has been asserted that more defections took place between 1967 and 1971 than during the first fifteen years. This was so because the different political parties welcomed defectors to retain the majority, which was so essential to keep themselves in power.

The coalition government also failed to follow any clear-cut policies. Most of the time these government continued to make compromises on various principles and failed to take any definite steps or actions because they were more concerned with their existence and survival rather than carrying out set principles or policies. The internal bickering and political strife's between the coalition contributed to the instability of their government and adversely affected the efficiency of administration.

However, it would be wrong to say that coalition politics has not left any good impact on the politics of India. One of the major effects of coalition politics has been that it has promoted compromise in politics and checked radicalism. It also relieved the government of the restraints and responsibilities which are imposed on the ruling party by the opposition benches under the party system. It has also been said that the coalition between the Akali Dal and BJP in Punjab resulted in welcome reduction in Hindu Sikh tension.

In a number of states the regional political parties have grown so powerful that they have succeeded in ousting Congress from power and forming their own government. The success of Akali Dal in Punjab, AIDMK in Tamil Nadu etc. The style of functioning of the Congress as a national party and as the ruling party at the centre also contributed for the development of regionalism in India.

Statement of the Problem

At the institutional level India's parliamentary federal structure provides the basic framework within which national and state or regional political parties can coexist. The distribution of the powers between the centre and states offer incentives to set-up state parties. However, as long as India was a centralised federation the Congress dominated it, once the federation began to loosen up, a multiplicity of parties emerged in the states. The rise of regional political parties was partly a natural development and partly a reaction to over centralisation by crucial national leaders and Congress government in the 1970's and 1980's. Over centralisation produced a counterweight, the federalisation of the polity and formation of new regional and state based political parties.

The decline of the Congress party and one party dominance system and with the emergence of various new political parties at various level, regional political parties have gradually assumed a lot of significance in Indian political system. Coalition governments have become an inevitable and indispensable part of national and regional politics in the present scenario of India. India has been experimenting with various coalitions at the national level since the last three or more decades.[2] Regional political parties have been constructed for the purpose of forming the coalition governments and also to oppose and depose the existing governments at the central level as well as state levels.

However, the emergence of strong regional political parties like DMK, TDP and Akali Dal have brought about a significant change in the coalition politics at the national level. The strong coalition governments, which came into existence under the banner of National Front, United Front and NDA-led BJP, UPA I and II governments respectively have done a lot of good in the direction of strengthening the federalism and decentralisation of political power.

The United Front government in 1996 and later installation of the BJP-led government both in 1998 and 1999 the survival of the BJP-led NDA government at the centre had depended on the support of the regional parties. In 2004, UPA – I and in 2009 UPA-II governments were formed with the support of regional parties. On all these occasions the role of Tamil Nadu regional political parties is very significant.

The regional parties shared power at the centre, which changed their outlook. They made the common approach to major policy matter a 'common minimum programme' document according to which the central government was to operate. Political scientists and leaders have been debating the possible impact of regional parties in Indian political system, but the fact remains that they have come to stay even at the national level and play a very significant role. More than anything the regional parties have demonstrated time and again, that they have come to play a decisive role in the national government.

This shows that, the recent political scenario regional political parties have been playing significant role in national coalition politics. In this work an attempt has been made to analyse the role of regional parties in Tamil Nadu in making and unmaking governments at the centre.

Significance of the study

The role of regional parties in making and unmaking of central government is very significant in the present political conditions in the country. The rise and fall of central government in the present context depends on the regional political parties. The study helps us to know the growing importance and role of regional political parties in Indian politics and their working in the Indian party system. The study is very relevant to present situation.

Objectives of the Study

1. To examine the causes for the emergence of regional political parties in India and their importance in national politics.

2. To examine the role of regional political parties in coalition government.

3. To examine the causes for the emergence of regional parties in Tamil Nadu.

4. To study the role of regional parties of Tamil Nadu in national coalition politics.

5. To examine the role of regional political parties with reference to Tamil Nadu in making and unmaking governments at the centre.

6. To suggest measures to strengthen the working of coalition politics and party system in India.

Hypotheses

1. The process of fragmentation of the Indian polity is not over but continuing.

2. The polity is not becoming bipolar with smaller parties, including regional parties and caste-based parties, having no choice appendages of either the BJP or the Congress either before or after elections.

3. The decline of the Congress has not automatically resulted in the rise of the BJP in other words, the political tussle between the two largest political parties in India has not been a 'zero sum game' in which the losses of one inevitably result in the other gaining by filling a so-called political vacuum.

4. Coalition policies is maturing. Political parties are becoming increasingly adopt at managing contradictions and are now even able to co-exist at the Union level with major rivals in the states. The electorate too seems to better understand the compulsions of coalition politics that lead to alliances appearing contradictory or even illogical.

5. The fate of national government depends on the support of regional parties, therefore in this era of coalition politics interdependence between national parties and regional parties has become inevitable.

6. The coalition formed with the support of regional and national parties with differing ideology can sustain for a full period of five years in the midst of pull and pressures due to localism, and will it be possible for such coalition to achieve growth, development, peace and integrity of the nation.

Methodology

The whole study of Indian regional parties involves historical, descriptive and analytic method. Historical approach has been adopted depending upon documentary sources like the Live Telecast of regional politics discussion have been viewed regularly, further the interview of regional political parties experts also seen to have a kind of glance of various regional politics in India as well as Tamil Nadu this kind of information has been recorded in the form of description.

The data has been collected from secondary sources such as the books, articles, national and international journals, dissertations, abstracts, seminar and conference papers and news papers etc. Hence the present study depends partly on primary and partly secondary sources.

Limitations of the Study

The present work is limited to the study of role of regional political parties in Indian Coalition parties, there are number of national and regional political parties in India. But present studies confined to the role of regional political parties of Tamil Nadu in Indian Coalition politics.

Scope of the Study

The scope of the present study is limited to probe the origin and growth of regional political parties in India in general and

Tamil Nadu in particular. The role of regional political parties in India in general and Tamil Nadu in particular is the main subject theme of present study. The study also offers suggestions to strengthen the working of Coalition politics.

Review of related literature

A good number of scholarly works have been written on political parties and coalition governments during the 20th century based on the experiences of Britain and the European countries. But the classical works have been mostly based in favour of single-party majoritarian governments and they have regarded multi-party governments as non-durable. More objective and comparative transitional studies appeared towards the end of the century and they seemed to take the coalition phenomenon as natural and related to political culture. The growth of the scientific interest in the study of European coalition politics led to the development of two approaches; the European politics tradition and the game-theoretic tradition. The chief contributor to the latter tradition has been William Riker whose Theory of Coalitions (1962) has become the source of the theory of minimum winning coalition.

Lawrence C. Dodd challenges the time-old theory that a durable cabinet (Coalitions in Parliamentary Government, 1976) requires a majority party government and argues for a fundamental alteration in the existing conceptions. Vernon Bogdanor [Coalition Government in Western Europe (ed.), 1983] describes the working of coalition governments in the democracies of Western Europe. The influence of coalition politics of Cabinet, Parliament, policy outputs, etc, are studied here in the context of countries like West Germany, Norway, Sweden, Denmark, the Netherlands, Belgium, Italy and Ireland. Lan Budge and Hans Keman (Parties and Democracy – Coalition Formation and Government Functioning in Twenty States, 1990) analyse the actual behaviour of some four hundred governments in twenty post-war democracies and try to find answers to questions relating to the formation of governments, distribution of portfolios and how parties influence policy. Michael Laver and Norman Schoefield (Multi-party Government the Politics of Coalition in Europe, 1990) have tried to reconcile the theoretical and empirical approaches to the study. Their work offers an accessible approach that bridge the distance between the 'European politics' and 'game theory' tradition of political science. Five basic themes are examined; the identity and motivation of actors in the game; the eventual membership of the coalitions they form; their durability; the pay offs that are shared and the impact of constitutional, behavioural and historical constraints on the process of coalition bargaining. Jug Steiner's comparative analysis (European Democracies, 3rd edition, 1995) is another major contribution in this area. Joseph M. Colomer's edited volume (Political Institutions in Europe, 1996) contains several sections on the individual nations and Europe. Jan-Erik Lane and Svante O. Ersson (European Politics: An Introduction, 1996) explains the character and trends of European politics and devotes a major part of the work for the analysis of European coalitions. Bradley Richardson's work (Japanese Democracy, 1977) pays attention to the recent coalitional developments in Japanese politics and thus takes a look towards Asia.

About politics in India, innumerable books and articles have been published. But specialist works on coalitional aspects, theory or practice have been limited in number. A few works deserve mention K.P. Karunakaran's edited volume (Coalition Governments in India: Problems and Prospects, 1975) analyses some theories and concepts about coalition making and gives brief reports about some States in India. S.C. Kashyap's edited work (Coalition Government and Politics in India, 1997) broadly examines the question in the context of the United Front coalition at the Centre. D. Sunder Ram's work (Indian Parliamentary Opposition (ed.), 1996) contains two reprinted articles on coalition politics in India, by Iqbal Narayan and Ramkrishna Hegde written much before coalitions appeared at the Centre. Indian Politics at the crossroads (1998) edited by Anil Kumar Jana presents three chapters dealing with the different aspects of coalition politics. Many articles have been published in various journals dealing with current politics of the country.

There are a few works on coalition in the Indian States including Kerala, West Bengal and Karnataka. John P. Jonh (Coalition Politics in Kerala, 1983) examines the working of the coalition ministries of the 1950's and 1960's. K.V. Vargese (UF Government in Kerala 1967 – 69, 1978) makes an exhaustive study of the coalition led by E.M. Sankaran Namboodripad in 1967-69, E.J. Thomas (Coalition Game Politics in Kerala after Independence, 1994) looks at coalition politics from the game theory point of view. A Balakrishnan Nair (Government and Politics of Kerala, 1994) makes a comprehensive study of Kerala politics including coalition phases. There are other writers, too, like T.J. Nossiter (Communism in Kerala: A Study in Political Adaptation, 1982), N. Jose Chander [Dynamics of State Politics – Kerala (ed.), 1986] who have paid attention to some aspects of coalition politics in Kerala. It may be noted here that some Ph.D. dissertations have been submitted to the University of Kerala which relate to some major aspects of coalition politics. Among them A.A. Sebastian's work (Role of Chief Minister in Coalition Governments: A Study of Kerala, 1994) and Raju Abraham's thesis (Role of Political Parties in State Legislature, 1990) are outstanding contributions.

Anjali Ghosh (Peaceful Transition of Power, 1981) makes a detailed and perceptive study of the coalitional games played by the Communists and non-Communists during 1966-1977 in West Bengal. P.R. Choudary's work (Left Experiments in West Bengal, 1985) deals with the political history of West Bengal during two decades 1960s and 1970s. Surabhu Banerjee's biography of Jyoti Basu (Jyoti Basu: The authorized Biography, 1997) covers the political developments of West Bengal from a biographical perspective. A number of articles have been published on Kerala and West Bengal in current journal and dailies, in addition.

However, no comprehensive and scientific analysis of the role of regional political parties of Tamil Nadu in Indian Coalition Politics has been attempted so far and the present work aims at filling this gap.

Research Design

The present study is structured and presented in the following seven chapters.

First Chapter entitled ***Introduction*** covers the Research Topic, Statement of the Study, Significant of the Study, Objectives, Hypotheses, Methodology and Review of Related Literature. Nature of Indian Democracy, party system in India.

Second Chapter deals with ***Evolution of Coalition Politics in India***.

Third Chapter explains about the ***Coalition Politics in the Context of Federal System in India***.

Fourth Chapter analyses ***Indian Coalition Politics and Regional Political Parties***.

Fifth Chapter assesses ***Coalition Politics at the Centre***.

Sixth Chapter deals with ***The Role of Regional Political Parties of Tamil Nadu in Indian Coalition Politics***.

Seventh Chapter deals with ***Summary and Conclusion***.

References

1. Bogdanor, Vernon (ed): *'Coalition Governments in Western Europe'*, London, 1983.
2. Dodd, Lawrence C.: *'Coalitions in Parliamentary Government'*, Princeton, New Jersey, 1976.

2

Evolution of Coalition Politics in India

Built on the majoritarian principle of the Westminster model and buttressed by the single-party dominance of the Indian National Congress, the Central and State Governments in India have been able to present a picture of stable parliamentary politics in the first two decades since Independence. However, there have been instances of States lacking in political stability from early 1950s owing to the failure of the major national party the Indian National Congress and of the regional parties to muster enough support to form a stable government.

The erstwhile States of Travancore - Cochin and PEPSU were the first two States in the country to form coalition governments after the first State Legislative Assembly elections in December 1951-January 1952. During 1953-67, three more coalition governments appeared: Andhra Pradesh (1953-56), Orissa (1957-62) and Kerala (1960-64). In 1967, eight States formed non-Congress coalition governments, and they were: Kerala, West Bengal, Punjab, Haryana, Uttar Pradesh, Madhya Pradesh, Bihar and Orissa. Of these States, Kerala, West Bengal, Punjab, Bihar and Orissa had fragmented Assemblies after the fourth general election of 1967. In Haryana, UP and MP, the Congress party formed its own governments but they fell owing to defection of members and gave way to coalitions. This trend continued although some of the above States went back to single-party Congress governments. In 1997, the number of States with coalition governments rose to fourteen, the States being: Kerala, West Bengal, Punjab, Haryana, Uttar Pradesh, Bihar, Maharashtra, Gujarat, Goa, Assam, Tripura, Mizoram, Manipur and Sikkim. In successive elections to the Parliament, the Congress party retained power at the Centre until 1977 when it was replaced by the Janata Party which was a hotch-potch union of several parties. The Centre also entered the coalition phase in 1996, having formed the first United Front government which was undoubtedly coalitional in character. Among the above States, Kerala has had the longest experience of stable coalition politics with West Bengal standing second. As their experiences have been unique in Indian politics their coalitional history has been examined in detail in separate chapters. Coalition politics of the other States have had a chequered history, going back and forth between single-party and coalitional forms of government. The experience of the major States are outlined briefly in the following paragraphs of this chapter.

Punjab witnessed the emergence of coalition politics in 1967 when the then ruling Congress party lost majority and the opposition parties formed a coalition government under the leadership of Gurnam Singh.[1] The constituents of the United Front were: Akali Dal (Master Tara Singh Group) 2: Akali Dal (Sant Group) 24; CPI(M) 3; SSP 1 and Independents 6. The CPI(M) gave unconditional support to the ministry without joining it. Starting with five ministers, the Cabinet was expanded five times to give representation to the constituents as well as to accommodate defectors from the Congress. However, internal dissensions within the leading Akali group and the manoeuvrings of the Congress from outside led to the rise and fall of four coalition Ministries during the period from 8 March, 1967 to 13 June, 1971 with a six months' President's rule and a mid-term poll in February 1969. The second phase of coalition government started after the June 1977 Assembly elections when the electoral alliance of Akali, Janata and CPI(M) parties captured 91 out of 117 seats. The Akalis and the Janata formed the government and the CPI(M) gave external support. This ministry led by Prakash Singh Badal came to an early end owing to infighting among the Akalis and withdrawal of support by the

Janata members on 3rd September, 1979 for reasons relating to the then Central Governmnet. The ministry continued until 17th February 1980 when it was dismissed and President's rule imposed together with eight other States in the wake of the Congress party coming to power at the Centre in January 1980. In the Congress secured 63 seats out of 117 and formed a government under Darbara Singh.[2] President's rule was imposed again in 1983, and the next polls were held in September 1985. In this poll the Akalis secured 73 out of 117 seats and formed the government. But this government led by Surjeet Singh Barnala had to face a serious crisis as 27 Akali members left the party and the government had to depend on the support of the Congress (I), BJP, CPI and CPI(M). However, in view of the fast deteriorating law and order situation in the State, the President's rule was declared again on 11th May, 1987.

After another spell of Congress(I) rule, marked by continued infighting of Akali factions and mass scale destruction of human lives, Punjab entered the next phase of a peaceful coalitional politics after the Assembly elections of February 1997. The Shiromani Akali Dal (SAD)-BJP electoral alliance won a near three-fourth majority and formed a coalition government under Prakash Singh Badal as Chief Minister. Although SAD alone has a strength of 74 out of 117, it has preferred to maintain the alliance in running the government for various political reasons. First, it was a pre-electoral alliance and was therefore committed to implementing a common minimum programme. Second, the BJP and the SAD are allies in the National Democratic Alliance at the Centre and have a joint responsibility to work together at the Centre for implementing the national agenda. Third, they have a common interest in sharing power at the Centre and in the State despite the apparently contradictory positions they occupy at the two capitals. The BJP's command over the SAD at the Centre and the superiority of the latter over the former in the State of Punjab make for a see-saw arrangement beneficial to both the parties. To sum up, the coalitional experiments in Punjab during the three decades since 1967 had been chequered by factional infighting in the major parties and the extremist violence let loose by terrorists and the police, resulting in the prolonged breakdown of law and order and the failure of constitutional government. Only when peace was finally restored in late nineties, could coalition politics of the Akalis and the BJP be established as a normal system of parliamentary government. However, the prospects of an alternative government-whether of a single-party or of coalition-do not appear bright in the present circumstances.

Bihar provided another instance of unstable coalition governments during 1967-72. During the five-year period the State had as many as nine governments with the life-span of four days to ten months.[3] Out of these governments, four were anti-Congress coalitions, three Congress-led coalitions and two Congress-supported minority coalitions. A mid-term poll was held in February 1969 which did not make any improvement on the situation. However, with the general elections in March 1972 the Congress (I) came back to power on its own, putting an end to the era of coalition governments. The second phase of coalition politics in Bihar started after the Legislative Assembly elections held in February 2000. The Rashtriya Janata Dal (RJD) - a breakaway wing of the former Janata Dal - led by Laloo Prasad Yadav and his wife Rabri Devi who was Chief Minister lost majority but gained the largest number of seats, ignoring the claim of RJD to be invited to form the government, the Governor V.C. Pande played politics to favour the NDA and invited Nitish Kumar who had been elected the leader of the NDA parliamentary party to form the government and prove his majority. However, Nitish Kumar had to make his exit within seven days as he could not win a majority in the Legislative Assembly. Although the Congress (I) and the Left parties had opposed the "corrupt" RJD government in the elections, they offered to support a "secular" RJD government to spite the "communal" NDA. Laloo Prasad Yadav cleverly supported the Congress (I) candidate for Speakership and checked the expected split in the Congress (I) by manipulating the absence of Congress (I) MLA's by keeping them in a Patna hotel.[4] The parties represented in the Assembly today are so fragmented as to foreclose any possibility of single-party government re-emerging.

The State of Orissa was one of the earliest to experiment with coalition government, having formed a coalition of the two largest parties in the Assembly, the Congress and the Ganatantra

Parishad in 1959.[5] After the second general elections in 1957 the Congress party had formed a government of its own under H.K. Mahatab as Chief Minister with the support of the Communists and the Jharkhand party. As problems arose between the Congress and the Communists, the former entered into coalition with the Parishad and formed the first coalition government on 12th May, 1959. The government continued to function for 21 months and finally broke down on 25th February, 1961 owing to factionalism within the Congress. The second coalition government came to power after the fourth general elections in 1967 when the Swatantra-Jana Congress government was formed with R.N. Singh Deo, the Swatantra Party leader, as Chief Minister. Split in the Congress in 1969 and the consequent changes in the relations between the Congress party of Orissa and the Jana Congress led to withdrawal of the Jana Congress from the ministry in January 1971.

The Assembly elections held in 1971 left the situation equally fluid although the Congress (I) emerged as the largest party. But a government could be formed by a coalition of the Swatantra Party and the Utkal Congress and supported by the Jharkhand Party. The Ministry was headed by Biswanth Das, a veteran Congressman who returned from political retirement. But the ministry broke down barely after 14 months, with the defection of some Swatantra members and the merger of the Utkal Congress with the Congress (I). Thereafter the State had a long spell of Congress rule, with a brief Janata interrugnum between 1978-80 and a Janata Dal government under Biju Patnaik until it was replaced by the fourth coalition government of Biju Janata Dal and the BJP elected in the Assembly elections of February 2000.

None of the first three coalition governments could complete a full term, and they broke down owning to intra-coalition conflicts or factional infighting within the constituents. The fourth government led by the Biju Janata Dal (BJD) and headed by Naveen Patnaik is cemented by the common interests of the BJP and the BJD who are also partners in the Central government and therefore depend on mutual support at the Centre and in the State.

The political situation in Uttar Pradesh was slightly different from that of the other States after the fourth general election. The Congress emerged as the largest party in the Legislative Assembly but it failed to secure absolute majority. However, the Congress managed to form a government of its own under C.B. Gupta as Chief Minister with the support of seventeen independent MLA's and four other MLA's who joined the Congress. But soon dissensions broke out in the Congress and Charan Singh, together with sixteen followers, left the Congress to form his own party, the Jana Congress. At the time of voting on the motion of thanks to the Governor's address, the Jana Congress voted with the opposition and defeated the government. On resignation of C.G. Gupta's Ministry, Charan Singh was elected leader of the opposition United Front and was sworn in as Chief Minister on 3rd April, 1967.[6] However, the government could not function smoothly, and MLA's started leaving the UF fold in batches until Charan Singh tendered his resignation on 17th February, 1968. The State was placed under President's rule and the Assembly dissolved.

Fresh elections were held on 9 February, 1969, and the Congress having secured majority in the Assembly, C.B. Gupta again formed the government on 26th February, 1969. Following the split in the Congress at the national level in 1969, some Congress MLA's led by Kamalapathi Tripathi left the Congress. Possibilities of a coalition government were explored but differences could not be settled regarding who was to lead a new government. After days of "bargaining games", Charan Singh who had by this time merged the Jana Congress with the Bharatiya Kranti Dal formed the second coalition government together with the Congress (I) on 17th February, 1970. The BKD soon fell out with the Congress (I) on several issues including nationalisation of sugar mills in the State and the abolition of privy purse by the Centre. The situation reached a breaking point when the Chief Minister asked thirteen out of twenty-six Congress ministers to resign and the latter refused. The Chief Minister then requested the Governor to dismiss the ministers, and the Congress in a countermove withdrew support and demanded the dismissal of the government. Although the Congress (I), Jan Sangh, Swatantra and Samyukta Socialist Party decided to extend support to the Charan Singh Ministry, the Governor recommended suspension of the Assembly and the proclamation of President's rule. And thus the second coalition came to an end on 1st October, 1970.

On the same day, the Congress (O), Jan Sangh and Swatantra Party agreed to form a United Legislative Party (Samyukta Vidhayak Dal) which was joined by the BKD in four days. The SVD thus came to have strength of 242 members in a House of 425, and elected T.N. Singh of the Congress (O) as their leader. After seventeen days of the President's rule, the SVD coalition under T.N. Singh came to power. As T.N. Singh was not a member of the legislature he sought election on 5 January, 1971 but was defeated by a Congress (I) candidate. However, he continued as Chief Minister until 30 March, 1971 when he tendered his resignation on the passage of an amendment to the official motion of thanks to the Governor. Several single-party Congress governments followed, with a Janata interregnum after the Emergency (1975-77). All political developments in UP were pushed under the carpet of history and politics stood still during the long spell of President's rule lasting from 1985 to 1997. The second phase of coalition politics in UP appeared when the elections were held in March 1997. The party position in the UP Legislative Assembly in 1997 was as follows:

Bharatiya Janata Party	175
Bahujan Samaj Party	67
Samajwadi Party	110
Congress (I)	37
Bharatiya Kisan Kamgar Party	8
Janata Dal	7
CPI	1
CPI (M)	4
Samata Party	2
Samajwadi Janata Party	1
Independents	13
Total Seats	425

Resource: ***The Hindu Daily News,*** 20th March 1997.

The President's rule continued until 21st March, 1997. Through a protracted process of discussions a novel political formula was devised between the BSP and the BJP to co-operate in spite of their being bitter enemies in the election. According to the formula, the Chief Ministership was to rotate between coalition partners – BJP and BSP – after every six months. The working of the ministry was to be monitored by a three-member panel comprising Vajpayee, Advani and Kanshi Ram. The first term of Chief Ministership was to be with the BSP and Speakership with the BJP. It was also agreed that the political situation would be reviewed by the two parties at the end of one year.

The ministry did not work smoothly, and a serious friction arose on the question of the change of Chief Minister and Speaker at the end of the first term of six months. However, it was decided to retain the Speakership with the BJP, and Kalyan Singh of BJP was sworn in as Chief Minister on 21st September 1997. The friction continued and the BSP pulled out of the government within a month. An unusual spectacle of horse-trading and defection followed which helped prop up the Kalyan Singh Ministry in power. Twenty-two out of thirty-seven Congress(I) MLAs formed the Loktantrik Congress Party and three out of seven Janata Dal members formed a separate group. Twelve rebel BSP members also joined the pro-Kalyan Singh camp. All defectors were rewarded with ministerships, raising the total number of ministers to 93 the biggest ever ministry in the Indian States. Although BJP could strengthen its hold on the government with artificial support encouraging defection in the opposition ranks, Chief Ministers had to be shifted to accommodate intra-coalitional conflicts and BJP's factional infighting.[8]

Uttar Pradesh has, thus, experimented with coalition governments, but governmental stability has been always undermined by the ulterior motives of power-mongering politicians. The trends established in the earlier phases are still maintained, resulting in frequent changes of ministries and their unscrupulous expansion. No serious efforts have been made to forge pre-poll alliances with any commitment to a common agenda; even the present ruling coalition is a post-poll, hotch potch arrangement. No institutional mechanism has been created to effectively co-ordinate the coalition partners or iron out their differences.

The State of Haryana, born on 1st November, 1966 out of the reorganisation of the State of Punjab, has been notorious for the defection games of its politicians. At the time of its formation the Congress party was able to make a government of its own under Bhagwat Dayal Sharma as Chief Minister who was reappointed as such after the Assembly elections of 1967.9 But differences arose within the Congress on the question of ministry formation, and the dissidents formed a new party – the Haryana Congress – and elected Rao Birendra Singh as its leader. The opposition parties collaborated with the Haryana Congress to form the United Front and elected Birendra Singh as the United Front leader. The latter was sworn in as the first coalition Chief Minister on 24th March, 1967. But as a result of frequent floor-crossings the relative strength of parties underwent changes and the Governor was compelled to dismiss the ministry on 21st November, 1967 and bring about President's rule in the State.

In the mid-term elections of May 1968, the Congress secured absolute majority and Bansi Lal became the Congress Chief Minister. But the game of defections continued and obstructed the functioning of the Legislative Assembly. Ultimately on the recommendation of the Chief Minister, the Governor dissolved the Assembly on 21st January, 1972. After the next elections held within three months, the Congress(I) could provide a single-party government which completed the full term. In the 1977 elections, the Janata party secured absolute majority and formed a single-party government. However, after the Congress victory in the Lok Sabha polls in 1980, it was not found necessary to dissolve the Haryana Assembly as the Chief Minister Bhajan Lal had moved to the Congress camp with enough followers could ensure a full term. The 1982 Assembly elections resulted in a fragmented situation wherein no party had enough majority to form a government.10 The Congress(I) and the Lok Dal-BJP combine staked their claims, and the Governor invited the Congress(I) leader Bhajan Lal to form the government. Bhajan Lal could complete the term without much interruption with the support of independents and defectors from the Lok Dal.

The second coalition ministry in Haryana came to office after the elections of June 1987 in which the Lok Dal (Bahuguna group) and its electoral ally BJP made a clean sweep.[11] Lok Dal had enough strength to form its own government, but Devi Lal who became Chief Minister included some BJP members also in the ministry. Instability of government continued to haunt Haryana from 1987 to 1991 when there were seven governments under five Chief Ministers. The next major coalitional development took place after the 1996 Assembly elections in which the BJP was an ally of the Haryana Vikas Party (HVP) led by Bansi Lal. A coalition government of the two parties was formed under Bansi Lal as Chief Minister. Inter-party conflict led to the withdrawal of support by BJP which rendered the government in a minority. Although the Congress (I) offered to prop up the HVP Ministry, they had to back out as Bansi Lal did not accede to some of their conditions.[12] Further a section of the HVP legislators broke away and helped the Indian National Lok Dal under Om Prakash Chautala to form a government in July 1999. In the February 2000 Assembly elections, held one year and a half ahead of schedule, the INLD fought in alliance with the BJP under the NDA banner and secured 47 and six seats respectively in an Assembly of 90 members in total. Although there are several points of conflict between the INLD and the BJP at the State level as well as at the national level, the alliance continues as a coalition government even after the elections.

Another major State where coalition government exists today is Maharashtra. In the Assembly elections held in September-October 1999 no party or combine could secure absolute majority. The BJP-Shiv Sena alliance which was ruling the State at this time was short of 20 seats to reach majority (Shiv Sena-69, BJP-56) in a House of 288.[13] The Congress (I) emerged as the largest party with 75 seats and the National Congress Party secured 58. The Congress (I) and the NCP had fought the elections independently and were enemies, the latter having broken away from the Congress (I) on the eve of the elections. However, after hard negotiations the Congress (I) and the NCP agreed to work together and form a coalition with the help of minor parties like the Peasants and Workers Party, Janata Dal (Secular), Samajwadi Party, Republican Party of India, Bahujan Mahasangh and the

CPI (M). The new coalition ministry took office towards the end of October 1999 under Vilasrao Deshmukh of Congress (I) as Chief Minister and Chhagan Bhujbal of NCP as Deputy Chief Minister.

The first coalition government of Maharashtra, formed by BJP and Shiv Sena, which ruled the State since 1995 had begun rather smoothly. But they developed intra-coalition conflicts and factional in fights within the Shiv Sena, leading to the replacement of the Chief Minister Manohar Joshi by Narayan Rane, both belonging to the Shiv Sena.[14] The present coalition includes two major partners who cannot be normally expected to work together, being factions of the same party and bitter fighters in the last election. But the attractions of power on the one hand and the alternative of losing it to a communal combine on the other forced the two secular parties - Congress(I) and NCP-to forge a post-poll coalition.

On the whole, out of the 28 States in India as on 1st January, 2001, 15 States have coalition governments and 12 single-party governments.

State-wise breakdown

States with Congress (I) Governments	*Other Single-party Governments*	*States with BJP Governments*
1. Arunachal Pradesh	1. Gujarath	1. Andhra Pradesh
2. Chattisgarh		2. Assam
3. Karnataka		3. Jammu & Kashmir
4. Madhya Pradesh		4. Sikkim
5. Nagaland		5. Tamil Nadu
6. Rajastan		

States with Congress (I) led Coalitions	*States with BJP led Coalitions*	*Other Coaltions*
1. Maharashtra	1. Goa	1. Bihar
	2. Himachal Pradesh	2. Haryana
	3. Jharkhand	3. Kerala

4. Uttaranchal	4. Meghalaya
5. Uttar Pradesh	5. Mizoram
	6. Orissa
	7. Punjab
	8. West Bengal
	9. Tripura

Having been formed by the combination of different variables and sub-variables, each coalition may have different characteristics. Based on an analysis of sub-variables, Iqbal Narian drew up a typology of coalition governments that existed in 1967.[15]

Coalitional Types by Sub-variables

1. By time sequence of coalition formation : Pre-election or Post-election	1. (a) Electoral alliance-turned governmental coalition. (b) Post-election governmental coalition.
2. By mutual strength of coalition partners	2. (a) One-Party dominant governmental coalition (b) Major-party dominant governmental coalition.
3. By strength of coalition partners vis-à-vis legislative strength.	3. (a) Majority governmental coalition. (b) Minority governmental coalition.
4. By ideological orientation of coalition partner.	4.(a) Ideologically homogeneous governmental coalition. (b) Ideologically heterogeneous governmental coalition. (a) Leftist governmental coalition. (c) Rightist governmental coalition. (d) Centrist governmental coalition. (e) Ideologically neutral governmental coalition.
5. By number of coalition partners coalition.	5. (a) Many party governmental (b) Two-party governmental coalition (c) Few-party governmental coalition

6. By interaction of infrastructure and politics	6. (a) Infrastructure dominated coalition (b) Secular coalition.

Based on the movement of coalitional politics through several stages of development, Iqbal Narain makes another categorisation[16]:

1. The phase of anti-Congress non-ideological coalition politics (1967-69).

2. The phase of anti-Congress programmatic coalitional politics (1969) from mid-term poll to the Congress split; and

3. The phase of politico-programmatic coalitional politics (1969-70) from the Congress split and after.

Jawaharlal Pandey has made a slight modification on Iqbal Narain's three-phased category in his analysis of Bihar politics by increasing the number to five[17]:

1. The phase of anti-Congress non-ideological coalitional politics.

2. The phase of anti-Congress ideological coalitional politics.

3. The phase of anti-non-Congress coalitional politics.

4. The phase of anti-Congress programmatic coalitional politics and

5. The phase of opportunistic coalitional politics.

As all the above phases are not applicable to all States in the country a more comprehensive and generally applicable phase-based categorisation may be adopted as:

1. Experimental phase.

2. Opportunistic phase and

3. Stability phase.

In every State's coalitional politics, political stability is finally achieved by passing through the earlier phases, whether prolonged or short. If the power game is well motivated and meant finally to achieve political stability, the opportunistic phase in which coalition partners use their clout for political bargaining may be viewed from a more sympathetic and more academic perspective. Opportunism and floor-crossing, in such a perspective, become strategies of identify-search, provided the political process ultimately results in polarisation and stability. The model is Kerala where a bipolarisation has developed between the LDF alliance and the UDF alliance leading to political stability. However, the political stability thus achieved need not necessarily be a permanent phenomenon inasmuch as a single-party stability cannot also be a permanent one.

Out of the fifteen States with coalition governments a few have achieved political stability through continuous experimentation and methodical practice on the part of the political parties and leaders (Kerala and West Bengal). A second category consists of States that have moved back and for the between one-party government and coalition without having the opportunity to practice coalition politics with commitment (Uttar Pradesh, Bihar and Goa). A third category manages coalitions under the patronage of anchor parties, i.e. one party having enough strength to run the government but willing to share some power with the poll allies (Haryana, Orissa, Punjab and West Bengal). The fourth category includes new entrants, still in the experimental stage (Maharashtra).

The fourth general election (1967) was believed to have marked a watershed in Indian politics, as it broke the Congress dominance in several States and aroused hopes of political polarisation.[18] But later developments resulted in the further fragmentation of party structure and gave rise to a more competitive multi-polar politics. The emergence of new political parties and forces including the regional parties occurred at the expense of the dominant Congress which was cut down to size in several States and subsequently at the Centre. Not only are the regional parties today cutting at the roots of the Congress power they are also checking the growth of any alternative party including the BJP at the national level. The two NDA and UPA experiments at the Centre strengthen the view that there is no going back to single-party dominance.

References

1. Dalip Singh: *Dynamics of Punjab Politics*, Macmillan, New Delhi, 1981, p. 93.

2. S.K. Khanna: *Coalition Politics in India*, Commonwealth Publishers, New Delhi, 1999, p. 26.

3. Jawaharlal Pandey: *State Politics in India*, Uppal, New Delhi, 1982, p. 14.

4. *Outlook*, 20th March 2000, p. 24.

5. R.N. Mishra: *'Patterns of Coalitional Politics in Orissa'*, in A.A. Padhi (ed.), *'Indian State Politics: A Case Study of Orissa'*, B.R. Publishing Corporation, Delhi, 1985, p. 39.

6. S.K. Khanna: *Op. cit.*, p. 39.

7. Lok Sabha Secretariat: *'Diary of Political Events'*, 1997.

8. Kalyan Singh was replaced by R.P. Gupta and later by Rajnath Singh, both of the BJP, as Chief Minister. Kalyan Singh organised another party after his suspension from the BJP.

9. Bhagwat Dayal Sharma assumed office on 10th March, 1967 and had to resign within two weeks.

10. The result was as follows: Congress (I) – 36; Lok Dal-31; BJP-6; JNP-1; Independents and others-12.

11. The election results: Lok Dal (B)-58; BJP-15; Cong. (I)-5; CPI-1; CPI(M)-1; Independents-6.

12. T.R. Rajalakshmi: *'Chautala Rides on'*, Frontline, 17th March 2000, p. 17.

13. The Hindu, Thiruvananthapuram, 10th October 1999.

14. *Ibid.*, 31st January 1999.

15. Iqbal Narian: *'Constitutional Politics in India and the Political System: The Crisis of Compatibility'*, reprinted in D. Sunder Ram (ed): *'Indian Parliamentary Opposition'*, Kanishka (New Delhi, 1996), p. 195.

16. Jawaharlal Pandey: *Op. cit.*, p. 29.

17. *Ibid.*, p. 29.

18. *Ibid.*, p. 40.

3

Coalition Politics in the Context of Federal System in India

In the federal-parliamentary democracy consists of an elected representative. Parliament which is supreme, a Cabinet collectively responsible to Parliament, a Prime Minister who is supreme within the Cabinet and an organised opposition within the Parliament. It was assumed that the majority would form the government and the minority would function as the opposition. Problems arose when no party could secure enough majority to form a single-party government, and in such circumstances the alternative was the coalition or multi-party government. This situation invariably leads to some changes in the traditional paradigm of parliamentary democracy. The composition of Cabinet, the nature of its working, the style of the Prime Minister/Chief Minister, the character of electoral politics and the party system, and even the composition of the legislature to a limited extent are likely to be affected by the nature of coalition politics. Although the UK had brief spells of coalition governments, they did not last long enough to change the institutional character. It is left to other countries that are compelled to work continuous coalitions to modify the parliamentary institutions.

Anglo-Saxon countries generally look at coalition government as an aberration, which on the continent of Europe it is the form. By the middle of 1983 only three European democracies - Britain, Spain and Greece - had single-party majority governments; the rest were ruled either by minority governments or by coalitions.[1] According to Bogdanor, it is hardly possible to understand European political systems without taking into account the working of coalitions. Accepted generalisations about Cabinet government, the role of legislatures and political parties all demand a fresh appraisal in the light of the exigencies of coalition politics. The processes of government formation and dissolution, the role of the Head of State and the working of the Cabinet are all likely to be affected by the coalitions, and the conventions regulating these processes may well differ from those operative in countries enjoying single-party government. In addition, strategies of political parties are likely to be affected by the knowledge that they will be unlikely to win power on their own but will have to share power with like-minded allies. The dynamics of a multi-party system in which coalition is the norm will, therefore, inevitably prove more complex than those in a system of the Westminster type with its presumption of two parties alternating in office, each in turn enjoying the full plenitude of power and patronage.

Coalition building between two or more parties has been frequent in Europe. Between 1990 and 1995 there were no less than 91 Cabinets in office, of which 19 were single-party governments, 69 multi-party governments and four caretaker governments.[2] Nevertheless they have not institutionalised coalition politics apart from the parliamentary system. Switzerland is the only exception in Europe with a permanent coalition government by means of its seven-member Federal Council, elected for a fixed four-year term by the Federal Assembly on a party proportional basis. Once the election results are known in Switzerland, it is a question of simple arithmetic as to how the Cabinet seats will be distributed among the parties. The process of Cabinet formation here does not create clear winners and losers.[3] As a result stability is very high in the Swiss case, especially since there exists no vote of non-confidence.

Parliamentarism reigns in Europe but varies from country to country as regards some basic structures and practices. According to Jan-Erik Lane and Svante O. Ersson, the institutions of parliamentarism may vary in relation to the legal requirements for:

1. Cabinet investiture or the procedure for appointing a Premier or government;
2. A vote of no-confidence by Parliament in relation to the government;
3. The request of a vote of confidence by the Premier; and
4. The dissolution of Parliament in order that new elections be held.[4]

In the UK there are few restrictions on how these four mechanisms of parliamentarism may be employed, whereas in other countries they are more regulated. The German requirement for a 'constructive vote of non-confidence' is one example, which is practiced also in Spain where Parliament is restricted to bringing down a government only if it can support a new one. Another instance is the French institution of the block vote, where the Premier may demand that a bill be voted on its entirety, and its rejection by Parliament entails that the Cabinet will step down. Finally, the prerogative of the Premier to dissolve Parliament may be restricted by rules that either stipulates specific circumstances, such as a successful motion of non-confidence, or place the final decision with someone else such as the President in countries with strong presidentialism.

Lane and Ersson distinguish between three types of coalition governments depending on how large the parliamentary support is.[5] They are:

1. Minority or less than 50 per cent support;
2. Small majority or more than 50 per cent and less than 60 per cent support;
3. Grand coalitions or oversized governments with more than 60 per cent support. The cut off point of 60 per cent in this classification is arbitrary.

In the Indian situation this may be raised to 67 per cent or two-third majority, as two-third majority is required for passing constitutional amendments. The minority model tends to prevail in the Scandinavian countries, whereas grand coalitions are to be found in the so-called consociational countries in Central Europe on the one hand and in the new democracies in Eastern Europe on the other.[6] Minority governments have existed in India both at the Centre and in some States, but majority governments have been the rule rather than the exception.

The level of political stability achieved in the post-1949 European democracies can be measured by the average life span of governments. According to an estimate, most of the elected Cabinets have survived for periods of considerable length.[7] The mean survival score in Germany has been 37 months and has been significantly higher than in Italy (13 months), Belgium (22 months) and the Netherlands (27 months). In most cases in Germany, the elected government remained in office throughout the period, but there have been exceptions to the rule, as in 1972 and in 1982 when a vote of confidence made way for the dissolution of Parliament before the full term.

Lawrence C. Dodd examines in his Coalitions in Parliamentary Government the arguments of eminent scholars from Lowell to Blondel who have asserted that coalition governments are bound to be short-lived.[8] A Lawrence Lowell had argued in his Governments and Parties in Continental Europe (1896) that "the parliamentary system will give a country strong and efficient government only in case the majority consists of a single-party". This thesis has been reaffirmed subsequently by several political scientists in their works. Lord Bryce says in Modern Democracies (1921) that a government formed by a coalition of parties is bound to be weak because of the unstable and conflicting character of the compromise involved. Harold J. Laski upholds, in Parliamentary Government in England (1938), that durable government requires a majority party system and argues that the multi-party system either results in a coalition with its "inherent corrosion of principles" or provides a minority government, which is likely to be weak. Maurice Duverger, in his Political Parties (1951) asserts that multi-partyism weakness the government in a parliamentary regime. The absence of a majority party necessitates the creation of heterogeneous Cabinets with "limited objectives" and "lukewarm measures".

Jean Blondel says that the duration of Cabinet governments is always influenced by the type of party system prevailing in the country and that one-party government is the factor contributing most decisively to the stability of governments.[9] He also says that coalition, small or large, appears directly antagonistic to stability. Scholars from Bryce to Duverger upheld Lowell's thesis by comparing the parliamentary experiences of France and Weimar Germany to those of the UK, implicitly accepting that the former were typical multi-party regimes while the latter was typical of a majority party system. Jean Blondel and Hans Daalder made an advancement by bringing more countries under examination. Blondel analysed the behaviour in seventeen Western parliamentary democracies from 1946 to 1966, focusing on the average differences in Cabinet durability between party systems; Daalder analysed ten smaller European democracies from 1918 to 1969. Several other writers too have contributed to the analysis of multi-partyism resulting in what Dodd calls "the myth of multi-partism" which implies:

1. Governments in multi-party Parliaments must be minority Cabinets, coalition Cabinets, or both;
2. Minority and coalition Cabinets are, by their very nature, bound to be transient; and
3. Multi-party systems are undesirable as they produce only transient governments.[10]

Dodd himself analysed the politics of seventeen European countries from 1919 to 1974 and observed: "While the durability of cabinets may be low for all multi-party parliaments, a large number of durable cabinets have survived in multi-party regimes."[11] He further says that while some multi-party Parliments produce durable Cabinets, other multi-party Parliaments produce transient Cabinets. This implies that durability depends not merely on the number of parties, but on a variety of factors. These factors are what constitute the political culture of a country. So whether a coalition government will be durable in a multi-party system or not depends on the political culture of the country concerned.

A coalition is an alliance of parties formed for the purpose of contesting elections jointly and/or forming a government and managing the governance by a process of sharing power. So coalition implies co-operation between political parties and this co-operation may take place at one or more of three different levels- electoral, parliamentary and governmental. Parliamentary coalitions occur, according to Bogdanor, when no single-party gains a majority and the party asked to form the government prefers to rule as a minority government on an understanding with another for external support.[12] Such an arrangement may be for a long period or for a limited period with a definite date of termination as with the Lib-Lab pact in Great Britain in 1977-78. It is also possible when a government seeks support from different parties for different items of legislation a method much used in Denmark where it is known as government by 'jumping majorities'. Finally, a minority government might survive without support on a basis of toleration by the opposition parties which do not vote it out for tactical reasons. This was in general the situation of the three Labour minority governments in Britain in 1924, 1929-31 and 1974. In Netherlands and Germany majority coalition rather than minority government is the invariable rule. In Denmark and to a lesser extent in the other Scandinavian countries, minorities may result from the process of government formation. In Italy also single-party governments have been formed and sustained by support from outside. Nevertheless in both Scandinavia and Italy majority coalition is almost always the preferred type. Japan too has experimented with coalition governments since 1993 and in spite of frequent changes of government majority coalition has been the order.[13] In India, the governments led by Charan Singh, Chandrasekhar and Deve Gowda had been sustained by Congress support from outside and that of V.P. Singh supported by BJP. In these cases the support had been issue-based as they claimed.

Electoral coalition is formed by two or more parties to fight the elections jointly against a common enemy. This may range from electoral alliance between parties at the national level to a mere understanding at the constituency level. Such coalitions need not necessarily last beyond the elections after which the parties may consider themselves free to make new alliances to form the government. The existence and nature of such coalitions will depend upon the character of the electoral system.[14] Certain electoral systems favour a coalition formation phase before elections rather than after them, a matter that has a fundamental impact on the politics of coalition.[15]

The governmental coalition is a "power sharing" coalition and it occurs when two or more parties, none of which is able to win a majority of its own, combine to form a majority government. The parties comprising such coalitions need not necessarily join together in an electoral pact; they may continue to compete electorally with their own coalition partners. This sort of power sharing coalitions are generally familiar to continental Europe, but comparatively unknown to British politics.[16] In fact, power sharing is the end of all coalitions and, therefore, it is the ultimate stage to be achieved in the election process. Any arrangement that stops short of the ultimate stage lacks commitment. Finally, there are what may be called 'integral' coalitions that link parties through the election process, parliamentary performance and governance. Continuous collaboration and cohesion of allies through the above stages of the political process make them constitute stable coalitions while preserving separate identity of the parties.

Vernon Bogdanor likes to look at coalition government as "a particular form of executive rule separate from both presidential government and from the classical model of Cabinet government as adumbrated by authorities such as Bagehot and Morely."[17] He asserts that a coalition government is more than a modified form of parliamentary government, having its own conventions and rules, all emerging from the fundamental principle of power sharing. According to him the impact of coalition government will be apparent throughout the whole of the political system, so that "the working of institutions such as the Cabinet and the legislature will prove very different from that of their counterparts in systems dominated by the Westminster Model." He points out some areas of government wherein coalition politics out some areas of government wherein coalition politics has made significant deviation from the Westminster model. These relate to the following:

1. *The role of the Head of State*: In a coalitional system the Head of State is always liable to find himself playing a more active role in government formation than is customary in Britain or in other countries where single-party majority government is the rule.

2. *Political homogeneity:* In a coalitional government ministers are invariably drawn from different political parties and hence they represent different and even contradictory viewpoints.

3. *Collective responsibility:* It is possible to maintain collective responsibility within a coalition Cabinet with the Prime Minister as the keystone. But it is harder to achieve this ideal in a coalition government than in a single party government.

4. *The role of the Prime Minister:* The Prime Minister of a coalition government is neither able to select his colleagues nor exercise control over them.

5. *The need for party discipline:* A coalition government is likely to be less able to afford breaches of party discipline than a single-party government. The coalition partners are bound by an agreement, tacit or open, on policy and performance, and dissenting votes by any backbencher may threaten the government's majority as well as the very basis of the coalition.

Many countries today have accepted coalition politics, but their constitutions are conspicuously silent on coalition governments which are derived from the exigencies of multi-party politics. Some constitutions, however, contain provisions which facilitate the formation of coalition governments. Germany is the most notable example which indirectly promotes coalition building by the constitutional provisions for a powerful Chancellor, constructive vote of no-confidence, regulation of parties, possibility of outlawing a disloyal opposition, etc. Coalition building in the Federal Republic of Germany was influenced by factors such as the political culture, the geopolitical situation of the country, the functioning of federalism and the development of large catch-all parties.[18] The Belgian Constitution provides for the equal representation in government, with the exception of the Prime Minister, of the French speaking and Dutch speaking members of Parliament.[19] The Constitution further says that on issues related to the language, legislation must be passed with a majority vote within each linguistic group of both Houses, provided the majority of members of each group are present and the total votes in favour of the two linguistic groups attain two-thirds of the votes cast. Apart from constitutional provisions, there are a number of other statutory and institutional factors in European States that might influence the formation of coalition politics, like the electoral system and rules relating to the formation and defeat of governments. A number of West European constitutions, for example, require that an incoming government should survive an investiture vote. This may be sometimes an informal convention; still it makes a major difference to the politics of coalition in a given system.

Coalitions may be classified as:

1. Policy pursuit models, and
2. Office seeking models based on objectives, and as
3. Minimum winning models, and
4. Large size models based on strategy.[20]

Policy pursuit models are those formed by like-minded parties, i.e. parties that have a common policy orientation or ideological background. It is often presumed that coalitions are easily formed to make a government when parties are not at a policy distance from each other. Examples are right wing coalitions and left wing coalitions. A coalition which combines leftist parties and rightist parties is a difficult proposition. But sometimes parties and individual legislators may be interested in the pursuit of power or office in total disregard of ideological considerations. They may argue that as power is an instrument for pursuing policies, power or office is what matters most in politics. Minor parties or uncommitted legislators may play truant and jump from the left front to the right front and vice versa, but they tend finally to settle down to a front that is more congenial to them.

William Riker's coalition model is office seeking and purely pragmatic. It involves two profound ideas. First, coalitions tend to be as small as is strictly necessary for winning a simple majority to form a government. A minimum winning coalition stands on the brink so much so that the defection of a single member will make the coalition no longer extant. Once advantage of a minimum winning coalition is that the total gains won by the coalition can be distributed in larger shares for each partner participating in the coalition. Hence it is a matter of maximum pay off for the minimum number possible. Second, minimum winning coalitions are less vulnerable to opinion shifts than grand coalitions or minority governments and therefore more durable than the latter. Probably being on the brink, a minimum winning coalition realises the necessity of discipline and cohesion among its ranks. However, the office seeking, minimum winning model is more theoretical than practical and it precludes the consideration of political reality or circumstances. In societies with sharp ethnic or other divisions and with innumerable groups and parties representing them, grand or large sized coalitions seem to be in order. In the Indian situation, both at the Centre and in the States, the tendency is to make coalitions large and broad-based and therefore the leading parties try to entice into their fold even feeble parties that are not sure of their post-election survival. Probably this is facilitated by three factors. One, the leading parties want to ensure such a large majority as to be representative of vast sections of people in the country. Two, the lack of discipline and cohesion among party legislators fail to assure the continuance of a minimum winning coalition. Three, the factional character of all parties, including the major parties, does not rule out the possibility of defection of members in spite of anti-defection laws that may exist in the country.

Most theoretical models of coalitional behaviour applied in Western Europe have tended to assume a bargaining environment more or less free from constraints. They tend to assume that every arithmetically possible combination has a chance of becoming real, other things being equal. Little or no attention is paid to the specific local circumstances or to the institutional, legal and personal constraints involved. Some constraints are products of very specific local circumstances like personality clashes, ethnic group identities or similar conflicts that deter groups or parties from coming together. In most political systems of Western Europe certain political parties have bargaining process by all other parties.[21] All such phenomena are available in the Indian society too, having a large and diverse population as in the whole of Europe taken together. Hence these constraints influence the character of coalitional politics in the national political system as well as in each State political system in the country.

In the light of the various studies conducted about the coalition governments of Europe, the Indian experience in coalition politics deserves to be examined. The Indian political system has similarities and differences with the European political systems in general, but the political culture and people being different the political outputs may also be different. Being the largest Parliamentary democracy in the world, India's experiments are of vital importance to the political world.

Impact of Coalition Politics on Parliamentary Institutions: The Indian Experience

India, having adopted a parliamentary structure of government within a federal system, has constitutionally provided for parliamentary structures at both the Centre and in the States. The same principles and norms of parliamentary practice are applied at both levels substantially. Innovations experimented and successfully operated at the Centre or in anyone of the States may be accepted as models or precedents by the rest whenever found useful.

It is largely the Westminster model of parliamentary structures that the Indian Constitution has adopted for both the Central and State governments. But the Indian political culture being different from that of the UK, the structures have had to be functionally modified. India being a vast subcontinent with innumerable culturally and ethnically diverse groups, political behaviour within the country has proved to be different from region to region or State to State. Ethnic loyalties and cultural diversities have tended to produce political behaviours different from each other, but within the same constitutional and legal framework. Therefore, although the legal framework is uniform throughout the country, political behaviour and practices tend to be different.

The constitutional system envisages a majoritarian form of parliamentary government in India at the Centre and the State, more or less like the British. However, the political reality has brought about multiple parties resulting in governments of party coalitions or alliances. The Congress party emerging from the national movement and seeking to represent a national consensus on political programmes and ideology wished to provide governments for the Centre and all the States for all time to come. But the majoritarian single-party governments became impossibility with the breakdown of the Congress and with the inability of the other parties to provide a single-party alternative being established. Although the Congress party has shown unwillingness to share power with other parties at the Central Government, it has permitted its State units to do so and thus participated in coalition governments early in the fifties. The Congress party of the erstwhile Travancore-Cochin State had been compelled to share power with the Tamil Nadu Congress and the Socialists in 1952 and in 1954. The political developments in Kerala since 1960 were results of coalition games centred on two major political parties - the Congress and the CPI (M). The communal equation had established the predominance of Nair and Christian communities in Travancore-Cochin State. The merger of Malabar and the formation of Kerala State shattered this equation and led to the considerable rise of Muslim and Ezhava power in the State. Thus, the change in communal equation produced its impact on the politics of the State and this appears to be the underlying factor of power politics in the State.

West Bengal was under Congress rule until 1967 when the party's grip was crippled and the Communists started rising in popularity. For one decade since 1967, West Bengal underwent a traumatic experience of governmental instability and political violence, and finally got settled under the leadership of the CPI-(M). Thus, while Kerala has been practicing coalitional politics for more than 40 years. West Bengal has experimented it for about 30 years and achieved stability since 1977.

The year 1967 marked a watershed in Indian politics as about eight States had formed non-Congress coalition governments.

The Congress dominance in Indian politics clearly broke in several States and the party had to sit in the Opposition. Although the Congress could regain power in some of these States, its popularity throughout the country was further eroded. The Congress lost power at the Centre within a few years and although it could come back in full glory it was doomed to lose it again. It lost control of more States in succeeding years so much so there were non-Congress coalition governments in fourteen States in 1997. The number of States that opted for coalition governments was increasing from 1967, but all States were not steady in the path of coalitions in this period. States like Rajasthan and Madhya Pradesh went back to Congress rule, while new States embarked on coalition experiment. Some States like Orissa, Maharashtra, Punjab, Bihar and Goa went back and forth between single-party rule and coalition rule. The steady decline of the Congress and the absence of another strong party to take its place either at the Centre or in the States in general has brought the coalition system to stay as a prevailing mode in the end of the 1990s.

The coalitional experience within the framework of Westminster model parliamentary structures, based on the present study, may be summed up as follows:

1. Coalition government in a parliamentary system are not necessarily unstable. Stability depends on several factors.
2. Coalition politics compel deviations and innovations in the parliamentary model to suit the needs of the coalition system.
3. The areas wherein coalition politics have made noticeable impact are broadly the Executive, the Legislature and the Party system.

Early writers used to presume that coalition politics undoubtedly led to short-lived governments, and they proffered statistics to prove the same. Their treatises failed to analyse the multi-dimensional causes involved and tended to make the inferences biased. E. Sreedharan points out four sets of factors that affect the stability of coalition governments.[21] First, the regime-level attributes or the institutional structures within which coalitions are formed. These include the fragmented character of the parties, the effective number of parties, the degree of ideological polarisation, the opposition's access to policy influence, the legal provision for elections in case of a government collapse and the provision for a constructive no-confidence vote as well as for a formal confidence vote after investiture. Second, the attributes of the coalition itself, such as the majority or minority status of the coalition, the number of parties in the coalition, its ideological cohesiveness, etc. Third, the nature of the ideological spectrum, that is, whether the coalition is ideologically single-polar, bi-polar or multi-polar. Fourth, the incidence of any political event that creates diverging reactions among members of the coalition. Gregory M. Luebert points to the kind of compromise reached between partners on the basis of their respective policy profiles as the key to stability.[22]

The above observations based on Western theories are presumed to be universalistic in character and application. But the Indian society and politics do not fit into the Western framework. In the Indian situation, the present study leads to certain inferences which may be listed as follows:

1. Coalitions cut across Left-Right, communal-secular national-regional divisions with the chief pursuit of office as the only reality.

2. Coalition between an anchor party and satellite parties tends to be stable.

3. Among such coalitions, if the anchor party commands a majority by itself as in West Bengal, it is likely to be stabler. A coalition of mutually dependent parties (that is, no party having a majority on its own) also is likely to be durable as in Kerala. Of the two categories mentioned, the former is likely to be stabler.

4. Minority coalitions, propped up by external support whether conditionally or unconditionally, are not likely to be stable.

5. The anchor party tends to make more than proportionate concessions to the smaller ones who gain more than proportionately to their strength.

6. Factions within the parties, particularly the anchor party, threaten the stability of the coalition.
7. Factional splits tend to be accommodated in the pursuit of office-seeking interest.
8. Surplus majority or large-size coalitions are stabler than minimal-winning coalitions.
9. Political cultures of Indian States vary, and some are more conducive to stable coalition politics than the others.

Impact made on the Executive, the Legislature and the Party System may be analysed separately with respect to each area and the consequences assessed.

The Executive

The three dimensions of the parliamentary executive that are influenced by coalition politics are: Cabinet formation, Cabinet management and the nature of the Cabinet. The institutional and legal, the political and personal dimensions of the Cabinet system get interlinked with the two basic processes of the parliamentary executive, viz. Cabinet formation and Cabinet management. The majoritarian Cabinet and the coalition Cabinet, being different as regards the above three dimensions, tend to produce different impacts on the two processes and their results. The Constitution envisages, as already pointed out, a majoritarian government of the British model and provides for a parliamentary government. Article 74 and Article 163 respectively state that there shall be a Council of Ministers with the Prime Minister/ Chief Minister as the head to aid and advise the President of India/Governor of the State in the exercise of their functions. According to the parliamentary practice, the leader of the majority party in the Parliament/State Legislature becomes the Prime Minister/Chief Minister and he in turn selects his colleagues in the Council of Ministers.

In coalition politics, the leader of the leading party is usually elected as the leader of the parliamentary party of the coalition, but he shall be acceptable to the allies as well. Sometimes the leader of a minority party may be chosen by the coalition to head the Cabinet. The general principle seems to be that the head of the Cabinet, whatever the degree of standing he has in his own party, shall be acceptable to all partners of the coalition whose will may turn out to be decisive in the matter of electing the Prime Minister/Chief Minister. It is, generally, observed that the general election to the Parliament or the State legislature is today the occasion for electing the Prime Minister/Chief Minister also, as the whole election process is centred round the leader of the party or alliance of parties. But in a coalitional set up the post-election situation can upset the earlier arrangements.

As regards the appointment of the Council of Ministers, Article 75(1) and Article 164(1) of the Constitution say that the Prime Minister/Chief Minister shall be appointed by the President /Governor and that the other ministers shall be appointed by the President/Governor on the advice of the Prime Minister/ Chief Minister. The traditional practice is that the Prime Minister/ Chief Minister will choose the ministers by paying due weightage to various factors to be considered. In coalition politics in India, the ministers are chosen by the respective parties themselves, and the Prime Minister/Chief Minister may not have a say in normal circumstances. This situation further weakens the position of the Prime Minister/Chief Minister in relation to his own party, particularly if it is ridden with factionalism. There are instances of Prime Ministers and Chief Ministers being dictated to by factions in their own party about appointing some members as ministers or even about avoiding the appointment of somebody whom they do not like to be with them in the Cabinet. This is possible in a single-party government also, but in a multi-party government the Prime Minister/Chief Minister is comparatively weaker.

Coalition is a bargaining process between the partners, and the process is on-going from the start to the finish. The representation of the partners in the ministry, the allocation of proportionate seats and the distribution of portfolios among them often occasion serious bargaining. It is admissible if the major parties get a bigger share as they can be supposed to have a bigger stake in election campaigns and a greater responsibility in administration. But it often happens in India that the smaller parties plead for a disproportionately larger pay off in terms of the number and importance of positions, and they often succeed in winning them. This is particularly so when the leading party is dependent on the minor parties for the maintenance of the coalition. The minor partners seem to presume that it becomes solely the responsibility of the leading party to preserve the coalition and they behave in irresponsible ways very often. So to say, the leading party becomes the loser in the bargaining game as it has to give up a party of its due share in order to satisfy the bullying partners. It must be surprising that in some coalitions, all MLA's of partner party are made ministers in order to prop up the ministry.

As regards distribution of portfolios there is always fight for 'plum posts' like Finance, External Affairs, Railways and Defence at the Centre and for similar prestigious portfolios in State Governments. Such distribution can be arranged to the satisfaction of all parties only by a process of negotiation and compromise. Compromise can be arrived at through inter-party discussions or discussions in the co-ordination committees. Issues like distribution of portfolios can be settled most effectively by co-ordination committees. Any discontentment left in this regard may crop up again and create fresh crises now and then which may even lead to destruction of the coalition. Hence distribution of portfolios is a very delicate task for the Prime Minister/Chief Minister in a coalition demanding astute handling.

The demand for larger representation and better portfolios is likely to create funny situations as regards the size of the Cabinet. The number of ministers may go on increasing as the 'accommodating spirit' waxes, and one may wonder if a poor country like India can afford to have so many ministers to govern them. On the basis of the recommendation of the Karana Singh Committee (1992) it was generally accepted that ministerial positions should not exceed one-tenth of the strength of the lower house concerned. But this has been violated by Chief Ministers like Kalyan Singh of UP and Rabri Devi of Bihar who offered to make ministers of all defectors in order to win their support to prop up the Ministry.[23] Members of the Lok Tantrik Congress party who formed the new party after crossing floor from the Congress (I) were all ministers in Kalyan Singh's ministry and later in R.P. Gupta's ministry. Some of them had only very minor portfolios or had no portfolios at all.

Once the Council of Ministers is formed, there arises the problem of co-coordinating them and pulling them together. As they belong to different political parties, the ministers may have different or even contradictory opinions, interests and visions. The foremost characteristic of a coalition ministry is the absence of political homogeneity. As such, the management of ministerial colleagues and monitoring of their activities call for extraordinary competence and patience on the part of the Prime Minister/ Chief Minister.

The Cabinet system of UK has historically evolved the character of collective responsibility. The Indian Constitution has legalised this character in Article 75(3) and Article 164(2) which state that the Council of Ministers shall be collectively responsible to the Lower House. 'Collective responsibility' implies that all ministers hold themselves responsible is formally taken by the Cabinet, each minister has the obligation to defend it publicity. Even if someone has a dissent with the collective decision, the dissenting view is expected to be suppressed or kept in reserve for the time. This aspect was emphasised by the Supreme Court when he latter expressed 'distress' and 'concern' over some statements of Ram Jethmalani, the Central Law Minister in Vajpayee's second ministry, which appeared contradictory to an affidavit filed in the court by the Government of India.[24] Jethmalani had to resign his post when he criticised the Chief Justice of India and the Attorney-General following the above observation of the Supreme Court. The Prime Minister had to admit in the Rajya Sabha that the Law Minister had to admit in the Rajya Sabha that the Law Minister was not willing to submit himself to the discipline of collective responsibility and that on a number of occasions he had spoken out on matters that did not pertain to his ministerial responsibilities.[25]

There are umpteen number of instances where in dissent has co-existed with collective responsibility in the various coalition governments. The CPI and the Forward Bloc in West Bengal could not agree with the new industrial policy of the CPI (M), but they decided to remain in government. In West Bengal the coalition partners had sometimes led agitations against the government of which they were a part. Further there were often intra-coalition dissensions in West Bengal and Kerala when one party was threatened by the growth of power on the part of another. On the eve of elections, they came to open clashes on the distribution of seats between them. In recent times the country has witnessed the PMK and MDMK ministers of the NDA government openly dissenting, with the Central Cabinet's collective stand on Sri Lanka.[26] Hence the concept of collective responsibility in its classical form needs to be made flexible in the coalitional structure of government. Political homogeneity being the first victim of coalition governments, an agreement to accommodate dissent becomes inevitable.

In majoritarian governments there is no institution other than the Cabinet to formulate policies and co-ordinate ministers or departments of government. The party machinery exercises control over the Prime Minister/Chief Minister and other ministers directly. But in a coalition Ministry consisting of several parties, there is no single-party machinery which can control all of them. Ministers belong to several parties and their future political prospects rest with their own parties. In such circumstances it is quite rational to evolve a separate forum for bringing the coalition allies together to discuss policy matters. In other words, institutionalised bargaining structures become relevant in coalition politics. However, there have been instances of the Co-ordination Committee becoming too powerful as a super Cabinet and interfering in administrative matters. As it is an extra-constitutional body of informal origin it is necessary to watch and control its growth so as not to infringe upon the constitutional status of the Cabinet. At the same time it is equally necessary to see that it is not neglected, as often complained by allies, and it has to be kept on an even keel. It is important that all coalition partners cultivate an attitude of respect towards the Co-ordination Committees. It is, therefore, advisable to provide for a constitutional status to the Co-ordination Committees in case of coalition governments.

The ideal of an all-party national government was suggested time and again, since 1989, in the context of a single-party failing to get majority in the Lok Sabha.[27] One of the suggestions envisaged the election of the Prime Minister by the Lok Sabha by means of single transferable vote from among candidates (not necessarily members of Parliament) who would secure support of at least 100 Lok Sabha members. The Council of Ministers would consist of representatives of all parties in proportion to their strength in the House. A common minimum programme acceptable to all or most parties should be placed before both houses of Parliament and approved. A no-confidence motion passed against the government should be effective only after the election of an alternative Prime Minister. Other suggestions included that:

1. The Prime Minister be elected by the Lok Sabha and shall resign only when an alternative leader is chosen.
2. The Prime Minister be elected by a majority of the Lok Sabha and Rajya Sabha.
3. The Prime Minister be elected by a majority of the Lok Sabha and Rajya Sabha and be removed only by 2/3rd majority in both houses; and
4. The Prime Minister be elected by a simple majority of the Lok Sabha and a no-confidence motion passed by 2/3rd majority of the Lok Sabha.

The above suggestions are meant to be applied in a multiparty situation where no single-party is able to form a government. In such a situation the choice of Prime Minister or leader of the coalition shall be determined by a process of member participation and not by the party caucus. But any amendment of the existing system shall be done without violating the spirit of parliamentary process. The present coalition system, not being anti-parliamentary or non-parliamentary, the most that can be advised to be done by way of constitutional amendment is to see that the Prime Minister is not removed without ensuring the election of an alternative leader to be sworn in.[28]

Coalition is the dexterous execution of a tight-rope balancing, involving compromise between two or more distant or even contrary stand points. The deciding factor may be the payoffs emerging out of the bargaining process. Since each partner wants to take more for itself and give less to the other partners in the coalition, the centrally located parties are at an advantage in coalition bargaining.[29] It may theoretically be argued that larger parties possess better bargaining power because of their conspicuous presence and leadership status.[30] But this is not always proved in practice and in the Indian situation smaller parties are found to be enjoying a disproportionately larger share in the arrangements. The leading party in the ruling coalition is often forced to part with its favourite choice to satisfy the smaller parties. And some of the latter like the AIADMK in the 1998 BJP-led government; the Trinamool Congress in the 1999 BJP-led government, or like the Muslim League and the Kerala Congress parties in Kerala which are prepared for a brinkmanship game extract larger chunks. Among the perks that the parties fight for are included not merely the ministerial portfolios, but membership of committees, membership of delegations and anything that shows off a higher status or superiority. In the present system of arrangements at the Centre, the BJP is at a disadvantage when compared to the other partners of the coalition. Out of the eleven committee Chairmen of the Lok Sabha the BJP has only one whereas the Congress (I), the leading party of the opposition, has two. And out of six Rajya Sabha Committees, the BJP has two Chairmen and the Congress (I) two in parliamentary delegations, the minor partners get more than proportionate number of representatives. It may also be noted that in the seating arrangements of the Lok Sabha, the BJP does not have a proportionate number of seats in the front row of the chamber.

Since the objective of the partners is to maximise their position and power within the government, it is presumed that they behave in a rational as it is presumed to be and as such, the durability of the coalition could be in jeopardy. The bargaining process is made more complex by the involvement of more players like factions within the parties themselves. This is made worse when two factions of the same party hold opposite views about joining a coalition.

Sometimes there may be mini-coalitions within the larger coalition and they may function with the objective of wresting out special favours for them. Special common interests developed by a few partners thus forming a mini-coalition run against the general interest of the government and may ultimately end up in the ouster of the government. The 'federal front' formed under the leadership of Chandrababhu Naidu within the United Front government, and the mini-front led by C. Achutha Menon in Kerala forming the government after the overthrow of E.M.S. Namboodiripad Ministry on 1st November 1969 exemplify this tendency.

It is sometimes observed that two political parties representing the same social divisions or having the same ideological roots may find it more difficult to form an alliance or coalition than for two parties representing different social bases.[31] But it is equally well said that like-minded parties, that is, parties having the same background or philosophy are likely to coalesce more easily than parties with differing background or philosophy. Both arguments hold good, although apparently contradictory, but the success of coalition making depends on the nature of bargaining conditions. And once the coalition has been forged, the social cleavages and ideological nearness do not matter.

The Legislature

Structurally, coalition politics has not brought about any change in the Parliament or State legislatures. The parliamentary functionaries remain the same, and the rules of procedure and conduct of business also do not change. There are as many parliamentary parties and whips as there are political parties represented; and there will be a joint parliamentary party for the whole alliance whether ruling or in opposition.

Committees will be constituted and monitored under the same norms as they exist in parliamentary practices. Bills can be passed if the required majority is forthcoming as per rules. Constitutional amendments may be severely hampered or pushed back when it becomes difficult to muster two-third majority without the backing of the opposition. When the coalition gains a two-third majority on its own, it has still the burden of carrying all the coalition partners with it.

In a parliamentary system of government, it was the Parliament that originated as the centre of power, the Cabinet being dependent on and responsible to the Parliament. As time taped, the Cabinet appropriated political power and importance. And the governmental system came to be described "Cabinet dictatorship". The growth of the importance of the Prime

Minister, centralisation of power in his hands and the consequent subjugation of the party and the ministers to the Prime Minister justified the sobriquet of "Prime Ministerial" government for the same parliamentary system. However, the changes were indicative of the trends in the paradigm shift of legislature executive relationship in the parliamentary system. The emergence of coalition politics and the consequent weakening of the Prime Ministerial position tended to effect a change in the role of the Parliament in relation to the executive.

The coalition partners, being participants in the government, are supposed to provide its solidity and be collectively responsible for its performance. But being different in origin and character, they often make for dissent and mutual criticism. Thus, a coalition government has also a built in mechanism for mutual checks and balances. However, the actual performance of coalitions deviate from the idealistic vision of smooth collaboration and friendly dissent. They sometimes break into open fights on the floor of the house and outside. Any observer of the conduct of business in the Lok Sabha will be struck by the behavioural contrast of the members during the Congress regime and the post-Congress coalition period. The incidence of unruly behaviour in both houses of Parliament has been more frequent during the latter, and the Speaker has been compelled to convene meetings of parliamentary party leaders more often than before to settle quarrels. This points to the absence of a centralised parliamentary party organisation in a coalition system when contrasted to a single-party majority.

From a sociological point of view, this phenomenon is reflective of a general decline in the elitist character of the people's representatives. Legislators speak in the language of the masses and behave in a style understandable to them. They come from the grassroots and represent the popular culture unlike the legislators of the fifties and sixties who represented a higher level culture. Moreover, with innumerable parties represented in the Parliament and State legislatures, the MP/MLAs feel themselves close to their respective party chiefs and immediately responsible to them unlike in the days of the Congress dominance system. The party chiefs behave like feudal lords and demand total loyalty from their legislators. The latter are dependent on their leaders for their career and future political existence. Today the legislator's freedom of speech in the legislature is restrained by the party leadership even though no legal provision provides for it.[32]

The Opposition may also be a coalition as in Kerala or it may consist of disunited single parties or groups of parties as in West Bengal or at the Centre. In either case one major function of the Opposition appears to be to entice the ruling coalition partners into their fold, not only to pull down the government but to strengthen their ranks. So the Opposition is never satisfied with attacking the policies of the government as in an orderly parliamentary system, but it is always alert on using other means for overthrowing the ruling coalition. Both sides being coalitions, it may be presumed that they are easily susceptible to efforts to make wedges in their blocs. Relatively, the Opposition of the coalition system at the Centre has become more powerful than that of the earlier Congress system.

The Party System

Coalition politics centres round political parties as it involves games played by the latter to gain the maximum pay off. It becomes relevant when no single party is able to reach power by itself. In such circumstances one party joins another one or more parties to fight the elections and / or to form a government. The word 'coalition' originates from the Latin word 'coalition' which means 'growing together'. Coalition is basically an alliance of parties that decide together. Coalition is basically an alliance of parties that decide to work together in the election process or after the elections and share power in running the government.

Coalitions or party alliances may be pre-election or post-election phenomena. Some parties may cluster together, pool their resources and work jointly to maximise their gain by defeating the rivals in the election process. If there is a single alliance fighting the rivals in parties, the possibility of the alliance winning more seats than the rivals is stronger. If two equally strong alliances are pitted against each other. The effect will be that of strong two party systems, either of them setting a majority to form the government. If more than two alliances contest, the result will be either in favour of one of them or none at all, with no alliance being able to win a majority. In the last situation, a government is possible only by means of a further coalition of two or more alliances.

1. Single alliance Vs. Disunited parties.
2. First alliance Vs. Second alliance.
3. First alliance Vs. Second alliance Vs. Third alliance.

In West Bengal, the Left Front alliance has come to be established as dominant in the State Legislative Assembly elections since 1977. In all successive elections after 1977 the Left Front remained united as a broad-based coalition whereas the Congress (I) – the leading party in the oppositions – had failed to forge an effective alliance. In Kerala, the almost total victory of the Saptamumani led by CPI(M) in 1967 against a disunited opposition convinced all parties of the need of an alliance for winning an election. Since 1967 no election was fought in Kerala without at least two alliances. In the 1970 election to the Legislative Assembly there was a Third Front in addition. However, the phenomenon of bipolarisation has appeared in Kerala politics with the emergence of two alliances – the LDF and the UDF – which may reasonably be described as a "two party system within a multi-party system". The two coalition model presented by Kerala State ensuring the possibility of alternative governments appears, theoretically, preferable to the single coalition dominance of West Bengal.

In the general elections to the Lok Sabha in 1996 there was a multi-cornered contest, with no strongly built alliance on the national scene. The BJP had a semblance of an alliance with three minor parties; the Congress (I) almost fought it alone; and the National Front and the Left Front could not agree on a Third Front. The result was a fragmented Parliament with none being able to form a government of its own. The BJP being the largest party was given a chance but they could not master enough support. The post-election efforts brought the NF and the LF together to form a United Front and stake claim to form a government with the outside support of the Congress(I). Thus the United Front led by Deve Gowda consisting of thirteen parties was a post-election coalition formed temporarily to keep the BJP out of power. The UF-Congress(I) collaboration could not last beyond one year and a half as there was no common interest between them, and they soon fell as under.

In the next, Lok Sabha elections of 1998, the BJP alliance had expanded, its base to include sixteen parties, most of them region-based. The UF consisting of thirteen parties while in power lost its cohesion and had no accepted leader. The Congress(I) was still hesitant about a national level alliance, but was a bit rejuvenated owing to the "Sonia factor". Comparatively, the BJP-led alliance was more strongly united and more regionally based than the other two, and the election results proved the same. The BJP was determined to continue the alliance, with necessary modifications, in spite of internal contradictions. The National Democratic Alliance was forged sufficiently early to prepare for the electoral confrontation in 1999. It is apparent that in the present vortex of political relations in India coalitions are unavoidable.

What is the role of policy in coalition politics? According to M. Laver, political parties make use of policy packages as store fronts to attract voters and the leaders may forget them once the election is won.[33] Riker and Laver do not consider policy even as an instrument in electoral politics and coalition formation.[34] Anthony Downs said that parties formulate policies in order to win elections rather than win elections to formulate policies.[35] However, that a well-drawn-out policy and an air of commitment to implement the same will help maintain long term credibility of the party or coalition of parties is nowhere doubted.

Coalition involves a commitment on the part of the political parties concerned to implement a pragmatic common programme, however, much ideologically at poles they are partners should agree on a common minimum programme of action, the implementation of which becomes the objective of sharing power. This involves 'ideological compromises' on the part of radical and fundamentalist parties. Sometimes rightist and leftist parties come together to stall a common enemy. Or it may be a coalition of secularists and communalists of even of Marxists and anti-Marxists. In either case there must evolve a common programmes for positive action. The negative objective of pulling down a government or preventing a party from coming to power cannot succeed in bringing about a coalition. When 'like minded parties' or parties with similar ideological goals make a coalitions, the making of a common programme may not have serious setbacks. Serious problems occur when ideologically polarized parties are forced to work together. The common minimum programme becomes a common manifesto for all parties that join the coalition. It cannot be the sum total of all the manifestos of the individual parties which may include contradictory ideas and promises. The common minimum programme (CMP) manifests compromise and the minimum that the partners agree upon.

With a view to accommodating the ideologically distant parties, many ideological or 'fundamentalist' sacrifices will have to be made by the leading parties. Long standing coalitions will recognise the importance of CMPs and prepare them sufficiently early to face the elections. Hurriedly patched up coalitions often make hotch-potch agreements, without deep understanding between them, to forge a common programme like the National Agenda of the UF of 1996 or of the BJP-led coalition of 1998. According to Ajay K. Mehra, the Dave Gowda government had developed a CMP which was based not only on the manifestos of the coalition partners, but also incorporated the political agenda of those parties which had not participated in the government.[36] The CMP was only a broad statement of approaches to deal with India's problems. The BJP-led coalition of 1998 elections thought of framing a CMP after the elections and set-up a drafting committee with George Fernandez as convener for the purpose.[37] The document, called the National Agenda and prepared by Govindacharya, a General Secretary of the BJP, under direct inputs from Vajpayee, Advani and Fernandez, sought to avoid the polities of confrontation and usher in an era of national reconciliation and consensus.[38] The BJP sensed the growing returns from appearing moderate and accommodating. The BJP had to change its stance on some contentious issues like reconstruction of the Ram Temple at Ayodhya, introduction of a Uniform Civil Code and the deletion of Article 370 which gave special status to the Jammu and Kashmir State. These items were serious led-down for the BJP which had tried to build up the party organisation on this plank. Moreover, the AIADMK which was an ally in the election refused to give a letter of support to the BJP to form the government until some of its unreasonable demands were incorporated into the agenda.[39] The AIADMK leader Jayalalitha had put forth five conditions:

1. Dismissal of DMK government in Tamil Nadu.
2. Central Finance Ministry to go to Subramanian Swamy.
3. Implementation of Cauvery Tribunal Award immediately.
4. Making Tamil an official language, and
5. Allowing states to have their own reservation policy.

She also wanted to be put on the agenda a demand for raising the height of the Periyar dam in Kerala to 150 feet. In such circumstances the process of preparing the CMP could be an impossible task. However, preparation of the CMP is also a strategy of making the partners acceptable to each other.

In the 1998 elections to the Lok Sabha the UF brought out a CMP and a joint policy statement on behalf of its partners, but the Left parties issued a separate manifesto highlighting their differences with the UF.[40] In Kerala State, in the 1967 Legislative Assembly elections, the seven-party Left Democratic Front had adopted a minimum programme for the first time and continued the practice in all successive elections. The UDF also followed this practice and launched minimum programmes collectively. However, in the Assembly elections held in 1996 some of the coalition partners launched their individual programmes in addition to the common minimum programmes. This creates the interesting situation of the coalition projecting the minimum programme collectively and the maximum programme individually. This also reflects a lack of total faith in the coalition system as such.

In a single member constituency multiple party system, small parties are not able to attain power by themselves and therefore they try to latch on to bigger party for the purpose. In a single member constituency system particularly, small parties fail to grow beyond their pockets of influence and their appeal is limited to their vote banks. So, in order to expand their sphere of influence or power they have to ally with other parties. At the same time each party is constrained by the other parties from growing into the areas of the latter. Thus, coalition gives an opportunity for growth as well as it put limits to growth. One party may try to break the limits by encouraging splits in other parties and weakening them. Internal splits destroy the parties themselves in the long run, but the split groups are accommodated for the time without destroying the coalition. The internal split of a coalition party, even when promoted by other coalition partners, may be treated apparently as an internal matter of the party concerned. The tendency to accommodate split groups help the smaller parties thrive in a coalition at the cost of the parent party and they get disproportionate political leverage.

Personality – based factions and parties are a common phenomenon on the Indian political scene. This provides personality clash any alliance between cause for party splits and in such cases any alliance between two newly emerging personality centred parties becomes almost impossibility, despite policy closeness or similarity of social base. Bitter hostility between the rival leaders and their followers may force close a meeting point, as in the cases of Karunanidhi Vs. Jayalalitha, Laloo Prasad Yadav vs. Ram Vilas Paswan and Ramakrishna Hegde Vs. Deve Gowda. But a common enemy or the lure of office may bring them together into the same coalition or another coalition after a lapse of time. Kerala State has witnessed a number of party splits resulting from personal ego conflicts as also their existence within the same coalition in view of remaining in office. The Kerala Congress is split into four parties, and three of them remain in the UDF as partners and one in the LDF. Ram Vilas Paswan has made his exit from the Janata Dal (U) – a partner of the NDA Ministry – and yet he collaborates with the parent party led by Sharad Yadav and remains in the NDA Ministry today.

Party coalitions in India always try to expand their base by attracting more parties than required for keeping themselves in power. That is, in other words large sized coalitions are a matter of attraction in the Indian situation. Following the tradition of the Indian National Congress in accommodating a large number of groups and interests, the party coalitions tend to make themselves 'Maha-coalitions' for winning the largest number of seats for themselves and reduce the opposition to nil so the ruling coalition seem to be an constant search to pick and swallow from the opposition. At the Centre, a government can function effectively only if it is assured of two-third majority to make constitutional amendments possible. At the State level even a minimum majority can support the government in power and make it effective. Although minimum winning coalitions are applicable to State Governments, and not to the Central Government, the general tendency is to accommodate large-sized coalitions in the States also. This is a characteristic reflective of the political culture of the country.

Another phenomenon in Indian politics is the non-participating external support that some parties prefer to offer in order to prop up a party or coalition of parties in power without making a commitment to share the responsibilities of government. Parties think ahead about the consequences of their participation as regards the forthcoming elections to Parliament or regional elections to the State Assembly as well as about other reactions in State politics. And if they find the pay offs from immediate power lesser than the latent pay offs in store for them, they naturally prefer to stay off from immediate power. This has been the policy of TDP and Trinamul Congress towards the NDA government. However, TDP was prepared to have a minimal participation by accepting the Speakership of Lok Sabha. This policy may result also from other covert considerations of the party leader such as stifling the growth of rival members in the party by blocking their entry into power positions. This further makes them feel free to declare their independence of the regime at slight prevarications.

The political culture- coalitional politics linkage in the Indian situation is clear from the observations made in the above pages. What may be called the Indian political culture is a composite of heterogeneous, State based political cultures further diversified by ethnocentric factors and evolutionary phases. The coalitional setup is a political power relationship evolved from an all inclusive, umbrella organisation of the Congress party and shaped by historical imperatives like the declining one party dominance and Marxian change of attitude towards parliamentary palliative. But the common cultural elements may contribute to the emergence of stable political arrangement in most States of the country, if not is all.

Finally, the dependence of coalition politics on the electoral system needs to be examined. Maurice Duverger evolved a three point thesis, from his analysis of European electoral politics, regarding proportional representation and the party system. The thesis included:

1. That proportional representation tends to lead to the formation of many independent parties.
2. That the two ballot majority system tends to lead to the formation of many parties that are allied with each there, and
3. That the plurality rule tends to produce a two party system.

Duverger's law has been examined at length, stimulating a whole body of research into the political consequences of electoral systems. But the impact of the plurality rule in the Indian situation has not been uni-dimensional or even bi-dimensional, being complicated by several factors such as ethnic divisions, economic cleavages and size of constituencies. The Italian experience of Proportional Representation compelled the revision of the electoral law in 1993, introducing plurality rule in three quarters of the seats for Senate and Chamber of Deputies while retaining proportionality for the other party.[43] The first elections held in 1994 after the adoption of the new law witnessed a trend towards three alliances – Left, Right and Centre. But in contrast to Britain and the US the Left and the Right were not unitarian political parties but loose alliances of very diverse parties. The experience of the Kerala State has been towards the creation and continuance of two alliances functioning more or less like a two party formation. The plurality system's seat vote disproportionality reinforces the stability of coalitions based on compromises. Disunity would mean to them vote disaggregation and disproportionate loss of votes.

References

1. Vernon Bogdanor (ed.): *'Coalition Government in Western Europe'*, London, 1983, p.1.
2. Lane and Ersson: *'European Politics: An Introduction'*, Sage, New Delhi, 1996, p. 137.
3. Jug Steiner: *'European Democracies'*, 3rd edition, Longman, New York, 1995, p. 73.
4. Lane and Ersson: *Op.cit.,* p. 104.
5. *Ibid.*, p. 138.
6. *Ibid.*, p. 149.
7. Manfred G. Schmidt: *'Germany – the Grand Coalition State'* in Joseph M. Colomer (ed.) Political Institutions in Europe, Routledge, New York, 1996, p. 74.
8. Lawrence C. Dodd: *'Coalitions in Parlimentary Government'*, Princeton University Press, New Jersey, 1976, p. 7.
9. *Ibid.*, p. 9.
10. *Ibid.*, p.10.
11. *Ibid.*, p.13.
12. V. Bogdanor: *Op.cit.*, p. 5.
13. Bradley Richardson: *'Japanese Democracy'*, Yale University Press, New Haven, 1997, p. 88.
14. V. Bogdanor: *Op.cit.*, p. 7.
15. Michael Laver and Norman Schofield: *'Multi-party Government – The Politics of Coalition in Europe'*, OUP, New York, 1990, p. 202.
16. V. Bogdanor: *Op.cit.*, p. 11.
17. *Ibid.*, p. 263.
18. Klaus Von Beyme: *'Coalition Government in West Germany'*, in V. Bogdanor, *Op.cit.*, p. 34.

19. Michael Laver and Norman Schofield: *op. cit.*, p. 202.
20. Lane and Ersson: *Op. cit.*, pp. 135-36.
21. D.D. Khanna (ed.): 'Principles, Power and Coalitions Politics in India, Lessions from Theory Comparison and Recent History' in D.D. Khanna (ed.), Principles Power and Politices, MacMillan, New Delhi, 1999, pp. 275-77.
22. *Ibid.*
23. *The Hindu*, Thiruvananthapuram, 22nd November, 1999.
24. *Ibid.,* Thiruvananthapuram, 22nd July, 2000.
25. Harish Khare: *'The Governance of Coalition Government'*, The Hindu, 30rd July, 2000.
26. *Ibid.*
27. D. Sunder Ram (ed.): *'Coalition Poltices in India'* NPH, Jaipur, 2000, pp. 253-54.
28. N. Jose Clander: *'Coalition Politics and Constitutional Reform'* in B.I. Fadia (ed.): *'Reviewing the Constitution'*, Himanshu, New Delhi, 2001, pp. 90-91.
29. Akhtar Majeed: *'Coalitions as Power Sharing Arrangements'*, in Akhtar Majeed (ed.): *'Coalition Politics and power sharing'*, Manak, New Delhi, 2000, p.7.
30. *Ibid.*
31. *Ibid.*
32. Raju Abraham: *'Role of Political Parties in State Legislature'*, New Delhi, 1999.
33. Akhtar Majeed, *Op. cit.*, p. 16.
34. *Ibid.*
35. Anthony Downs: *'An Economic Theory of Democracy'*, Harper Row, New York, 1957, p. 28.
36. Subhash C, Kashyap (ed.): *"The Cabinet system in a Coalition Situation", 'Coalition Government and Politics in India'* (New Delhi, 1997), p. 98.

37. *"The Pioneer"*, New Delhi, 15th March, 1998.
38. Swapan Das Gupta and Sabanaumi Bhaumik: *'Crown of Thorns'*, India Today, 16 March, 1998 p. 16.
39. *Hindustan Times,* New Delhi, 13th March, 1998.
40. *The Hindu,* 2 February, 1998.
41. A. Balakrishan Nair: *'The Government and Politics of Kerala'*, Thiruvananthapuram, 1994, pp. 168-69.

4

Indian Coalition Politics and Regional Political Parties

Elections are the cornerstone of democracy. They lie at the heart of the democratic process and are on expression of popular will. In fact, democracy is based on the active and intelligent interest of the people in their national affairs and the elections that result in the formation of governments.[1] Elections to parliament have been conducted in India since 1952 under the constitution. With a new hope, many political parties are coming up to participate in the power game. Emergence of numerous political parties in India is a gift of Multi-party system.[2] The recent elections to the Lok Sabha and Vidhan Sabhas while giving a very powerful blow to the national parties which has put up its most disastrous performance ever, have immensely enhanced the importance and role of the regional Political Parties in Indian Politics.[3] The country has seen more or less orderly electoral process covering 14 Lok Sabha elections. Especially the 10th, 11th, 12th, 13th and 14th general elections have witnessed the mushrooming of regional Political Parties and regionalisation of national Political Parties.[4] Because of national party had neglected to give adequate importance to their regional and state units. In the first two decades of independence the Congress party remained in power at the centre and some states as one party dominance though India has a Multi-party system.

Table –1

The Composition of Majorities in the Lok Sabha and Prime Minister

General Elections	*Composition of Majority*	*Prime Minister*
1st Lok Sabha (1952-1957)	Congress Party has two-thirds majority	Nehru
2nd Lok Sabha (1957-1962)	Congress Party has two-thirds majority	Nehru
3rd Lok Sabha (1962-1967)	Congress Party has two-thirds majority	Nehru, Shastri, I. Gandhi
4th Lok Sabha (1967-1971)	Simple (absolute) majority of the Congress Party	I. Gandhi
5th Lok Sabha (1971-1977)	Two-thirds majority of the Congress Party	I. Gandhi
6th Lok Sabha (1977-1980)	Simple (absolute) majority of the Janata Alliance BLD	Desai, C.C. Singh
7th Lok Sabha (1980-1984)	Simple (absolute) majority of the Congress Party	I. Gandhi
8th Lok Sabha (1984-1989)	Congress Party has two-thirds majority	R. Gandhi
9th Lok Sabha (1989-1991)	Congress Party has relative majority, but majority coalition of other parties is under leadership of Janata Dal	V.P. Singh, Chandrasekhar

(Contd.)

(Contd. Table-1)

General Elections	*Composition of Majority*	*Prime Minister*
10th Lok Sabha (1991-1996)	Congress Party has relative majority, but has coalition or agreements with smaller regional parties	Rao
11th Lok Sabha (1996-1998)	BJP has relative majority, but the minority government of United Front governs, supported in Parliament by the Congress Party	Vajpayee*, Gowda, Gujral
12th Lok Sabha (1998-1999)	BJP has relative majority, coalition government is under leadership of the BJP	Vajpayee
13th Lok Sabha (1999-2004)	BJP has relative majority, but BJP-led NDA (National Democratic Alliance) has absolute majority	Vajpayee
14th Lok Sabha (2004-)	UPA (United Progressive Alliances)	M.M. Singh

Source: Subhash C. Kashyap's Our Parliament p. 67.

* Vajpayee was named minister after his election to the leadership of the party holding the relative majority. However, since he could not attain a majority in the Lok Sabha, he resigned only days later to make room for the minority government of the United Front which had the support of the Congress-with first Gowda (until 1997) and then Gujral as prime minister.

The continuous hegemony of the Congress at the centre, led to neglect of the sentiments of the states. The Congress could not evolve a framework of democratic decentralisation in its party organisation, there was frequent interference of central leaders in matters like distribution of election tickets, formation of the ministry, selection of the State Unit Organisations. Defection is also one of the important factors at the national level as well as state level too. That many regional Political Parties are formed by defecting from their parent party for their selfish ends in the name of people's welfare. If any person were unable to get party tickets in the election they easily formed a separate Political Party but such regional Political Parties are born on the eve of election or near election time.[5]

The rising importance of regional Political Parties constitutes one of the most significant changes in recent Indian Politics. India's Party System has undergone a transformation over the last decades. The Congress Party a catch-all party that brought independence in 1947 and governed India for much of the period since then, no longer dominates the electoral scene. From the first election in independent India in 1952, until the fourth general election 1967, the Congress Party dominated not only the Lok Sabha but also state assemblies.[6]

During this period three general elections of 1952, 1957 and 1962 were held and Congress returned to power in almost all the states. In 1952, it won absolute majority in 18 out of 22 states, in rest of the four, it was the single largest party, while in 1957 it secured absolute majority in 11 out of 14 states and 1962, 12 out of 14 states. The party also enjoyed absolute majority in the parliament as well.[7]

But, the 1967, general election brought change in the political map by throwing off the monolistic control of the Congress rule in India. There was a shift from national Political Parties to regional Political Parties.[8] The Congress failed to secure majorities in eight states, and majority at the centre was reduced to a narrow margin of 54 per cent of seats. These results radically changed the political map of India marking the end of "One Party" dominance. This election had created a situation according to Rajni Kothari, in which "Congress dominance was subjected harsh judgement by supporters and opposition alike.[9]

The elections were variously interpreted as a swim to the right and swim to the left. Actually, there was no regular pattern in the defeat of the Congress in the States. The regional Political Party like dusk came to power in Tamil Nadu with an absolute majority. In Kerala, a communist-led United Front was decisive. Disparate coalitions of opposition parties formed shaky government in Kerala, West Bengal, Orissa, Bihar and Punjab. Later on, due to defection from the Congress, Uttar Pradesh, Haryana and Madhya Pradesh also had coalition governments, as a result of no party obtaining a majority of seats in the state legislature. It was phase of unstable governments in the states a precarious government at the centre, indecision in government policy and growing violence, all this a consequence of the decline of the Congress System.[10]

The monopoly of the Congress forming a single-party government at the centre and in most of the states was first challenged in 1967. But more formally and formally in 1977. The Indian National Congress(O), the Bharatiya Lok Dal, the Bharatiya Jan Sangh and the Socialist Party merged informally and formed the Janata Party. They also had an electoral understanding with the CIP(M).[11] The monopoly of the Congress party was broken at the centre for the first time and the Janata Party which wrested power with the support of regional political parties at the centre. Non-Congress governments were installed in a large number of states as well, with the thumping majorities.[12] But two years later the alliance crumbled.

After the grand experiment of coalition governments especially with the collaboration of regional Political Parties, many state governments were constituted. It was a unique event in Indian Polities after 1977, that any non-Congress Party came to power in any state even communists and Bharatiya Jan Sangh, came on a common platform, for the common cause of anti-congressism. Janata Party was a first grand experiment of coalition by the collaboration of regional Political Parties, who had marged in Janata Party.[13]

In the Lok Sabha of 1980 the Congress Party re-emerged in the power at the central level, 1980's were marked by on other significant development i.e., in some of the states regional

Political Parties captured power with their own distinct views and ideologies. The Telugu Desam Party in Andhra Pradesh, Kranti Ranga in Karnataka and Assam Gana Parishad came to power in Assam. The tension, conflicts and confrontation between the centre and states became more pronounced when different Political Parties captured political power at the centre and States.[14]

When Mrs. Gandhi came to power, she dismissed under Article 356 nine state governments ruled by Janata Party, as a reaction of Janata Party's dismissed of seven state governments. Though the Janata Party had dismissed them since their tenure of five years had expired, the Congress did it as a reaction subsequently; elections took place in these states. While Congress came back to power in many states, still in number of states including Andhra Pradesh, Tamil Nadu, Jammu and Kashmir, Karnataka and West Bengal non-Congress government were formed where regional Political Parties came to power, the TDP, DMK, National Conference, Janata Party and CPI(M) governments respectly. In 1984, NT Rama Rao's government was dismissed by the governor Ram Lal to install Congress government which was presented to by all opposition parties (and after a month NTR again became the Chief Minister). This was blow to the anti-Congress system. TDP, permanently became an enemy of the Congress. Similarly, the Shironami Akali Dal became a permanent enemy of the Congress Party.[15]

Hence, by the 1980s we had the creation of a "Political Vacuum" in some states leading to the entry of regional Political Parties[16]. Andhra Pradesh, Karnataka and Assam provide good examples of this phenomenon. The 1980s have hence seen the rise of parties which claim to have an altogether different programme from the Congress Party and do not seek to provide a national alternative to the Congress; rather they are rooted in regional grievances and aspirations.

The uneven or lopsided pattern of economic development in India since independence in which some regions have experienced faster economic development has also contributed to the rise of regional Political Parties.

Irrespective of the Indira wave of 1984 in which many opposition stalwarts, like former Prime Ministers Atal Behari Vajpayee and Chandrashekhar, lost their Lok Sabha elections to the light weights of the Congress, Telugu Desam Party in Andhra Pradesh managed to get 30 Lok Sabha seats and became the largest parliamentary opposition party in Lok Sabha.[17]

The cumulative outcome of November 1989 election was a "hung" Lok Sabha with no single Political Party commanding a majority on its own. It was a situation comparable, to a limited extent, to the situation which arose twenty years earlier when, following the split in the ruling party in 1969, the bigger Congress faction led by Prime Minister Mrs. Indira Gandhi did not command a majority in the fourth Lok Sabha. The government was able to continue with the support of Lok Sabha, elected in 1967, was relatively brief the ninth Lok Sabha "hung" from start.[18]

After the 9th Lok Sabha election in 1989, no Political Party could get a majority to form the government. Though the Congress Party emerged as a single largest party in the election but it did not stake its claim to form the government. The National Front which emerged as the second largest party, elected V.P. Singh its leader, and was invited to form the government by the President R. Venkataraman with the outside support of left parties and the BJP. Thus, as a result of the 1989 Lok Sabha election, the country witnessed the first minority-cum-coalition government at the centre.[19]

After the fall of V.P. Singh-led coalition government, the dissident leader Chandrashekhar staked his claim to form the government with the outside support of Congress (I), AIDMK, BJP, Muslim League, National Conference, Kerala Congress and a few independent Members. It was like a small party supported by a very large one from outside.

In 1991 elections to the Lok Sabha no party was in a position to secure a majority. The Congress got 225 seats and emerged as a single largest party. The BJP came second with 119 seats. P.V. Narsimha Rao formed his minority Congress government which nevertheless lasted nearly five years. It also had to depend on support of AIDMK, IUML, JMM Party etc., apart from capitalising

Table -2

Parties Position in Lok Sabha – 1996

Sl. No.	*PARTIES*	*SEATS*
1.	Janata Party (BJP)	160
2.	Congress	139
3.	Janata Dal	45
4.	Communist Party of India Marxist CPI (M)	32
5.	Tamil Manila Congress (TMC)	20
6.	Samajwadi Party (SP)	17
7.	Telugu Desam Party (TDP)	16
8.	Shiv Sena (SS)	15
9.	Communist Party of India (CPI)	12
10.	Bahujan Samaj Party (BSP)	11
11.	Samata Party (SP)	8
12.	Shiromani Akali Dal (SAD)	8
13.	Revolutionary Socialist Party (RSP)	5
14.	Assam Gan Parishad (AGP)	5
15.	Congress (T)	4
16.	Forward Block (FB)	3
17.	Haryana Vikas Congress (HVP)	3
18.	Muslim League (ML)	2
19.	Madhya Pradesh Vikas Congress (MPVC)	2
20.	Jharkhand Mukti Morcha (JMM)	1
21.	Assam Autonomous State Demand – Committee	1
22.	A.I. Majlis Ittihadul Musalmeen	1
23.	Maharastravadi Gomantak Party (MGP)	1
24.	Kerala Congress (KC)	1
25.	Sikkim Democratic Front	1
26.	Karnataka Congress (Bangarappa)	1
27.	United Goa Democratic Party (UDP)	1
28.	Independents Vacancies	3
	TOTAL	**543**

Resource: *Ahju, Election and Electoral Reforms in India (2000).*

(The ruling United Front consists of JD (45), CPI(M) (32), TMC (20), DMK (17), SP (17), TDP (16), CPI (12), AGP (5), Congress(T) (4), FB (3), RSP (5), MPVC (2), and KC (1) totalling – 179.)

on the splits in opposition parties, particularly in the Janata Dal, TDP and JMM. Thus the Congress government that existed during 1991-96 was also a coalition government for all practical purposes. Its depend on the regional parties and the other splinter groups was very crucial for its existence and survival.[20]

The 1996, general election once more resulted a "hung" parliament. No Political Party got a clear majority to form the government. Regional Political Parties played an important role in the formation of the government at the centre for the first time.[21] In the 1996 elections, the BJP emerged as the single largest party with 160 Lok Sabha seats and the Congress came second 139 seats. The President invited the BJP to form a government, which was done but this government could last for 13 days only. However, immediately after the installation of the BJP-led government, several Political Parties had organised United Front Government with the support of Congress (I) came to power, thus the government of 13 Political Parties composed of Janata Dal, Communist Party of India (CPI), Communist Party of India (Marxist) CPI(M), Assam Gana Parishad (AGP), Forward Block (FB), Dravid Munnetra Kazhagam (DMK), Tamil Manila Congress (TMC), Congress-Tewari, National Conference (NC), and Indian Union Muslim League (NML). The leader of the United Front H.D. Deve Gowda who was appointed Prime Minister himself was a regional leader. He was chosen by the leader of Telugu Desam (TDP) and Chief Minister of Andhra Pradesh Chandrababu Naidu. The Congress, however, did not like Deve Gowda to continue as the Prime Minister.[22]

With the fall of Deve Gowda government, another United Front coalition government led by I.K. Gujral assumed power at the centre. Except for the TMC Ministers initially the Gowda team itself became the Gujral team. The Congress after the getting of the price of Deve Gowda's head, further extended its support to Gujral Government from outside[23]. However, the Gujral Government also did not last long and also it later on withdrew its support on the plea of Jain Commission Report. During June, 1996 to March 1998, coalition politics remained operational. As part of the United Fronts, regional parties like the TDP, DMK and AGP became very active and played a key role, both in decision-making as well as in the selection of the leader of the coalition.

The 1998 election again produced a "Hung Parliament". No single Political Party got absolute majority. The BJP again emerged as the single largest party with 180 seats and the BJP-led alliance emerged the largest bloc in the Lok Sabha. But it fell shot of absolute majority in the Lower House of the parliament. The Congress emerged as the second largest party in the Lok Sabha with 141 seats. The United Front suffered most in this elections. Although the left parties, led by CPI(M), managed to hold their fort, the Janata Dal suffered a disaster. The CPI(M) and CPI won 32 and 39 seats, while Janata Dal got only six seats. The main cause of Janata Dal's election failure was the division of the party in Bihar, Orissa and Karnataka. In Bihar, Laloo Yadav's Rastriya Janata Dal (RJD) did reasonably well (17 seats). The Biju Janata Dal (BJD), in alliance with BJP, fared very well in Orissa. The Lok Shakti in Karnataka and

Table - 3

Three Major Alliances and their Seats in 1998

BJP		***Congress***		***UNITED FRONT***	
BJP	**– 182**	Congress	– 141	CPM	– 32
ADMK	– 18	RJD	– 17	CPI	– 9
SAP	– 12	RPI	– 4	RSP	– 5
BJD	– 9	IUML	– 2	FB	– 2
SAD	– 8	RJP	– 1	DMK	– 6
TL	– 7	UMF	– 1	TMC	– 3
SHP	– 6	KC (M)	– 1	JD	– 6
PMK	– 4	Independent	-1	Congress(S)	– 1
MDMK	-3				
LS	– 3				
JP	– 1				
HVP	– 1				
TRC	– 1				
HLD(R)	-4				
AC	– 2				
TDP	– 12				
JKC	– 3				
Independents	- 2				
Total	**– 278**	**Total**	**-168**	**Total**	**– 64**

Source: *Ahuja, Election and Electoral reforms in India, (2000).*

Samata Party in Bihar, in alliance with BJP did quite well in the election. It may be pointed out that RJD and Samata Party in Bihar, Lok Shakti in Karnataka and BJD in Orissa were some time back, parts of the Janata Dal. The important regional political parties like Lok Shakti, Samata Party, Trinamool Congress TDP and AIADMK got 3, 12, 7, 12 and 18 seats respectively.[24]

The 12th Lok Sabha was constituted in March 1998 and the largest party in the house, the Bharatiya Janata Party, was invited to form the government. However, the Atal Bihari Vajpayee led coalition government is running at the centre with the support of 18 other Political parties–both national and regional. Mr. Vajpayee, wizened by his earlier experience of 13 days in power, valiantly struggled to keep his flock together. But the shenanigans of his coalition partners, notably the AIDMK, kept the Vajpayee dispensation on the tenterhooks for 13 months. Other coalition partners, too pitched in with their demands asking for their pound of flesh. Mrs. Mamata Banerjee of Trinamool Congress wanted nothing but the best for West Bengal, the Akalis showed their displeasure over the Udhampur issue but did not choose to press their differences of opinion to the breaking point though Haryana's Indian National Lok Dal, led by Mr. Om Prakash Choutala, which choose to walk out of the coalition over the likes in rationed food articles, cooking gas and urea, returned to the fold at the last movement. The AIDMK Supremo continued exercising pressure over the BJP-led government over one issue or the other– whether it was the sacking of the Karunanidi-led-DMK government in Tamil Nadu or the distribution of Ministries at the centre. Enough embarrassment was caused to the government when the Shiv Sena and its volunteers tried their best to prevent the Pakistani cricket team from playing in India.[25]

The political uncertainty gripped the nation as the 13-month old BJP-led Coalition, led by Mr. Atal Bihari Vajpayee, bowed out of the power on April 17, 1999 when it lost vote of confidence in Lok Sabha by just only one vote (269-270).[26]

As a prelude to pulling out of the BJP-led coalition, AIADMK Chief Ms. Jayalalita decided to withdraw her support from the Vajpayee government.

However, one of the most important features of the 1998 general election was participation of as many as 176 political parties out of them only seven were national parties rest of 80 were registered state political parties and 89 were registered unrecognised political parties.[27] Apart from this, the focus of attention of almost all political parties were the pre-and-post-poll alliances. The 12th Lok Sabha also witnessed the phenomenon of which parties could be broken up and what alliances could be put up either to remain in power or to come to power.

The 13th Lok Sabha was India's another "hung" parliament. Where there is a "hung" parliament, and coalition government, the role of regional Political Parties is very significant. In 1999 the 13th Lok Sabha election, as many as 169 Political Parties were in the fray, out of which only seven were national parties (BJP, BSP, INC, JD(U), JD(S), CPI, CPM and 40 regional parties and the rest of 122 were registered unrecognised parties. In this election regional parties captured 26.93 per cent by winning 158 seats from the different states mostly from southern states. Other registered unrecognised partied captured 3.22 per cent by winning 10 seats and independent candidates got 2.74 per cent by capturing six seats, while National Parties got 67.16 per cent by winning 369 seats some important regional political parties that captured large number of seats in this election were TDP-29, SAP-26 seats, later it merged with JD(U), SHS-15 seats, DMK-12 seats, AHDMK-10 seats, BJD-10 seats, AITC-8 seats. Regional political parties have been taking a considerable share in ministry formation. Moreover some regional Political Parties have been dominating state election and formed location governments in states like TDP in Andhra Pradesh, AIADMK, DMK, MDMK in Tamil Nadu and National Conference in Jammu and Kashmir.[28]

In the North-Eastern States, 34 Political Parties were in the fray in the 13th Lok Sabha election for the 25 Lok Sabha seats including Sikkim. Out of the these, six National Parties (INC, BJP, JD(U), CPI, CPM and seventeen regional parties like Arunachal Congress, National Congress Party, United Minorities Front of Assam (UMFA), Federal Party of Manipur (FPM), Manipur People's Party (MPP), Manipur State Congress Party (MSCP), Hill State People's Democratic Party (HPDP), People's

Table – 4

Alliance of Political Parties in 1999

Party BJP + Allies 302	*Seats Won*	*Congress + Allies 136*	*Seats Won*
BJP	182	Congress	114
TDP	29	AIADMK	10
JD(U)	21	RJD	7
Shiv Sena	15	Muslim League	2
DMK	12	Kerala Cong. (M)	1
BJD	10	Kerala Cong. (J)	1
Trinamool Congress	8	Others	105
INLD	5	Left Front	
PMK	5	CPI (M)	33
MDMK	4	CPI	4
SAD	2	RSP	3
HVC	1	Others	3
LTC	2	Samajwadi Party	26
MGRADMK	2	BSP	14
National Conference	4	National Congress Party	7
		Rest	15

Source: *Deccan Chronicle,* April 16th 1999.

Democratic Movement (PDM), United Democratic Party (UDP), Lok Shakti (LS). All India Trinamool Congress (AITC), Sikkim Sangram Parishad (SSP) and other registered unrecognised parties were also in the fray. With a view to strengthen themselves some regional parties outside the region extended their units to the region.

The probable role of regional political parties in 1999, elections and thereafter, its role in government formation is concerned, it is very clear that they played a key role. Some key players and leaders of the regional political parties like Jayalalita and Karunanidi changed their former alliances. Regional stalwart of Gujarat, Waghela's party merger with Congress certainly affected at least to some extent the poll prospects of BJP. Sharad Power's NCP also hampered the victory opportunity of the Congress in Maharashtra. It certainly helped BJP-Shiv Sena alliance. We have already seen the continuous growth of regional

Table – 5

Party Position in the 14th Lok Sabha

Congress and Allies		*BJP and Allies*		*Left*		*Others*	
Congress	145	BJP Bhartiya Janata Party	138	CPI(M) Communist Party of India (M)	43	SP Samajwadi Party	36
RJD Rashtriya Janata Dal	20	Shiv Sena	12	CPI Communist Party of India	10	BSP Bahujan Samaj Party	19
DMK Dravida Munnetra Kazhagam	16	BJD Biju Janata Dal	11	AIFB All India Forward Bloc	3	JD (S) Janata Dal (S)	4
NCP Nationalist Congress Party	9	SAD Shiromani Akali Dal	8	RSP Revolutionary Socialist Party	3	NC National Conference	2
PMK Pattali Makkal Katchi	6	JD (U) Janata Dal (U)	8	KC (J) Kerala Congress (Joseph)	1	RLD Rashtriya Lok Dal	3
TRS Telangana Rashtra Samiti	5	TDP Telugu Desam Party	8	Independent	1	AGP Assam Gana Parishad	2

(Contd.)

(Contd. Table- 5)

Congress and Allies		*BJP and Allies*		*Left*		*Others*	
JMM Jharkhand Mukti Morcha	5	NTC Nationalist Trinamool Cong.	2			BNP Bhartiya Navshakti Party	1
MDMK Marumalarchi DMK	4	NPF Nagland People's Cong.	1			LISP Loktantrik Jan Samata Party	1
LJP Lok Janashakti Party	3	MNF Mizo National Front	1			MEIM Majilis-E-Ittahadul Muslimeen	1
PDP J&K People's Democratic Party	1	IFDP Indian Federal Democratic Party	1			NLP National Loktantrik Party	
RPI (A) Republican Party of India (A)	1					SDF Sikkim Democratic Front	1
Muslim League	1					SJP (R) Samajwadi Janata Party (R)	1
						Independents – 3	3
Total	**216**		187		61		**75**

Source: *The Hindu, New Delhi, May 14, 2004.*

political parties in terms of votes and seats since 1989 election. But one new thing happened in this election. It was the clear cut polarisation of various regional parties (baring some) either in favour of BJP-led NDA or in favour of Congress-led front. Even ideology and cadre based communist parties are also compelled to put themselves behind Congress alliance. It is one of the crucial shifts in Indian Political System. We have already seen the realignment of opposition forces since 1967 in the name of anti-Congressism. Now it is clear that the days of dominance of Congress Party is over. It can also be categorised as two party dominance system with the help of regional political parties.[29]

The 13th Lok Sabha was dissolved, at the advice of Prime Minister Vajpayee, almost eight months before the expiry of its term and when the Government was fully in command of a very comfortable majority. In fact, this is the first general election since 1977 that has upset every electoral calculation and poll prediction. No pollster or party leader of any significance thought of a verdict in which the Congress, not the Bharatiya Janata Party, would emerge as the single largest party in the 14th Lok Sabha. Out of 539 seats, result of which was declared on 13 May 2004, Congress and its allies won 216 seats, BJP and allies got 187, the left got 61 and 75 seats were won by others, including SP and BSP. Congress-led alliance, United Progressive Alliance (UPA), ended up 30 seats ahead of BJP-led combine (NDA). The Congress and its allies as pre-election formation and the Left-parties together constituted a majority in the 14th Lok Sabha, eliminating the predictions of hung-Parliament.[30]

The verdict 2004 once again proved that the days of one party dominance are over and in future, the national politics, would be the sum total of state politics. Today, each State is a political system unto itself, with its own party system and political rhythm. The polls seem to have shown India to be a far more federal nation than before. It reflects nation's diversity resulting in numerous forces vying for political space. The outcome at the national level, therefore, becomes the some total of the State level verdicts. Any party wishing to win a national mandate has to weave its way through the different States and secure a verdict in each of them. The BJP did well in Madhya Pradesh, Rajasthan and Chhattisgarh; slipped a little (along with its ally Shiv Sena) in Maharashtra; and made substantial inroads in Karnataka. Its biggest losses have come in Uttar Pradesh, Bihar, Jharkhand, Delhi, Haryana and Gujarat. Contrary to Opinion and Exit Poll findings, the BJP did not fare significantly better than its allies. Over the past decade and half, the BJP advanced on the national stage party through raising its vote share and partly through striking alliances in every region with parties big and small. This time, three of the BJP's senior partners in key States suffered a spectacular debacle- Jayalalitha's AIADMK in Tamil Nadu, Chandrababu Naidu's Telugu Desham Party in Andhra Pradesh and Mamata Banerjee's Nationalist Triamool Congress in West Bengal. The Janata Dal (United) fared poorly in Bihar. The impressive performance of two allies, the Biju Janata Dal in Orissa and the Shiromani Akali Dal in Punjab, could not

Table - 6

A comparison of number of seats won by national parties and regional parties in Lok Sabha elections of 1991, 1996, 1998 and 1999

Party	*1991*	*1996*	*1998*	*1999*
BJP	120	161	182	182
INC	232	140	141	114
BJP+INC	352	301	323	296
Janata Dal	59	46	6	JD(U) 21 JD(S) 1
CPI+M	35	32	32	33
CPI	14	12	9	4
BJP+INC+ JD+ CPM+CPI	460	391	370	355
Regional parties*	36	85	90	105

Sources: G.V.L. Narasimha Rao and K. Balakrishnan, Indian Elections- The Nineties, New Delhi: Har Anand, 1999.

[*Regional parties included are AIADMK, DMK, TDP, AGP, Akali Dal, Shiv Sena, National Conference, Tamil Maanila Congress, Lok Shakti, Biju Janata Dal, Jharkhand Mukti Morcha, Haryana Vikas Party, Rashtriya Janata Dal, Trinamul Congress, Nationalist Congress Party. But all of them did not contest all the elections.]

compensate for the flopping of the alliance factor in the big States of the South and the East.

This process of reconfiguration of the political space has seen the vote and seat share of regional political parties or alliances go up, thereby making the system more pluralistic and competitive. This is reflected in the bigger electoral presence of state regional parties in national politics in the present situation. Regional Political Parties increased their share of Lok Sabha seats from 54 in 1991 to 167 in 1999, and their vote share from

Table - 7

Majorities in the State Parliaments in the Largest States in 2000

State	
Andhra Pradesh	Regional TDP (Telugu Desam Party) has majority
Assam	Regional AGP (Asom Gana Parishad) has majority
Bihar	Regional RJD (Rashtriya Janata Dal) has majority
Gujarat	BJP has majority
Haryana	Regional INLD (Indian National Lok Dal) has majority
Karnataka	Congress Party has majority
Kerala	LDF (Left Democratic Front, including the CPM) has majority
Madya Pradesh	Congress Party has majority
Maharashtra	Alliance BJP (Hindu) Shiv Sena and smaller factions has majority
Orissa	Alliance BJP and the regional BJD (Biju Janata Dal) has majority
Punjab	Alliance BJP and the regional (Sikh) SAD (Shiromani Akali Dal) has majority
Rajasthan	BJP has majority
Tamil Nadu	Regional DMK (Dravida Munnetra Kazhagam) has majority
Uttar Pradesh	BJP has majority
West Bengal	CPIM (Communist Party of India / Marxist) has majority

Source: Ahuja-Election and Electoral reforms in India, (2000).

24 in 1996 to 30 per cent in 1999. This increase has taken place at expense of national parties, especially the BJP and the Congress, which have stagnated around 300 seats between them.[31]

The total number of seats won by regional parties in 1991, 1996, 1998 and 1999 Lok Sabha elections were 36, 85, 90 and 105 respectively. The significance of the number of seats won was increased manifold by the inability of major national parties, like the Congress, the BJP, and the Janata Dal to win a legislative majority in the Lok Sabha.

The fact that, the support of regional parties was necessary for the formation of a government at the centre bestowed on them a political significance disproportionate to the extent of their electoral victories.

In recent Indian political scenario, regional political parties are contenders for power in all states except Gujarat, Rajasthan and Madhya Pradesh.

Even the national parties could challenge it only in some states and not in the country as a whole.[32] For example, the Congress (I) Party, which is more of an all India character than other. But the Congress is not strong in Jammu & Kashmir, Punjab, Kerala, West Bengal and Tamil Nadu for long period. The Janata Party which emerged in 1977 as a National alternative in the wake of national emergency, could be represented only from eight out of 22 states in 1980, these states being Bihar, Gujurat, Haryana, Karnataka, M.P., Maharashtra, Rajasthan, U.P. and Delhi.[33] CPI, CPI(M) and other leftist parties only strong in West Bengal, Tripura and Kerala. The BJP also strong in Gujarat and Rajasthan.

Therefore, the role and importance of the regional political parties in India has thus grown to be strong force in many states, they are the ruling power and where they are not ruling power, they form significant force in the opposition.[34]

The number of regional political parties has increased markedly in the last few years, which is evident most significantly from the process of government formation at the centre. The installation of the BJP in power, could not have happened without the support of regional parties in the National Democratic Alliances (NDA).[35] And recent installation of Congress-led United Progressive Alliance is also supported from large number of regional political parties.

It is true that the activities of regional parties are confined to the concerned states or regions. At the same time, they have no capacity to form the government at the centre. Even then, their role is very significant in formation of the government. The role of regional parties, as the following instances make it very clear:

1. During the period of non-Congress system, if there has been any challenge to the Congress in electoral politics, it has always been from the regional political parties.[36] Though, the Congress was very dominant at the centre since the independence, yet after its first split in 1969. When 60 (out of 284) Congress members of the Lok Sabha crossed the floor and sat on the opposition benches; but that opportunity too was missed because, regional parties, like Muslim League and DMK lent support to Mrs Indira Gandhi's Government.[37]

2. The Congress (O), Jana Sangh, Baratiya Lok Dal, Janasangh and Socialist Party merged in Janata Party in 1977,[38] and headed by Sri. Morarji Desai was formed the government at the centre. Because, support of Akali Dal, DMK, CPI(M), Republican Party, the Peasant and Workers Party.[39] In 1979, it suffered a split and in its place Lok Dal became the ruling party as the Congress extended to it support from outside.

3. In 1985 and 1987, elections to state assemblies in Tamil Nadu and Jammu and Kashmir, M.G. Ramachandran, of AIADMK and Dr Farooq Abdullah, were able to secure absolute majority to form the government with their alliance.

4. In 1989, Janata Dal led by V.P. Singh, was able to form National Front Government, with the support of Congress(S) Telugu Desam, DMK and Assam Gan Parishad.[40] After the fall of the V.P. Singh-led coalition Government, the dissident leader Chandrasekhar staked his claim to form the

Government with the outside support of AIDMK, Muslim League, National Conference, Kerala Congress and a few independent members.[41]

5. In 1998, BJP was able to form the government, with the support of regional parties like AIADMK (18 MPs), Shiromani Akali Dal, Shiv Sena, Muthu DMK, Haryana Vikas party etc.

6. Similarly, in 1999 again BJP-led National Democratic Alliance was able to form the government at the Centre, with the support of regional parties like DMK, Telugu Desam, Trinamool Congress etc.

7. The regional parties extended full support to the central government to solve the problems of water and border disputes.

8. The regional parties also contested elections to the Lok Sabha and won seats. For example, Shiromani Akali Dal won eight seats, and AIADMK won 18 seats to the 12th Lok Sabha in 1998. These examples clearly indicate that, the regional parties have their due place in national politics.

9. The Coalition government to be formed, at the centre led by National parties invariably, depend on the support of regional parties. Otherwise, it becomes impossible for the National party, to form the government at the centre.

10. Regional parties, making, a strong demand for state autonomy, made the National parties, to include in their manifestoes, a provision for "state autonomy", so that, Centre-State relations are strengthened. For example,

    (i) In 1991, the National Front Manifesto said that it is "committed to true or genuine federalism, and will reverse over-centralisation brought about by Congress(I)".

    (ii) The Manifesto of CPI said (1991), "A strong centre is possible, when backed by strong states".

11. The regional parties, today, have broadened their base both in the South and North. It has resulted a interaction or proper balance between regional perspective and national perspective.

12. The fate of Central Government depends on the support of regional parties. For example, in 1999, the BJP government led by Atal Bihari Vajpayee fell, just by one vote, as Jayalalita, the leader of AIADMK, withdrew, all of a sudden the support of her 18 MPs.

The emergence and increasingly important role of regional political parties may be said to be a consequence of these reasons. First, India is virtually a land of many regions. The fact of diversity may be noted in respect of languages, customs, cultures and above all levels of the social and economic development. A powerful national political party like the Indian National Congress could give a set back to the destructive forces of regionalism by preaching as well as decline of this party, regional organisation naturally raised their head and managed to defeat the Congress in various states of the Indian Union.

Second, these regional organisations could successfully exploit the fact of local, regional and parochial grievances. The leader of the organisations could well thrive on the propaganda of 'regional imbalance' in respect of development caused by the negligent attitude of the centre.

Last, the rise and growth of such parties is also sustained by the existence of primordial loyalties by communal and ethnic forces. It is for this reasons that the regional leaders fail to broaden their area of operation to other parts of the country. Such regional parties thrive on exploitation of the regional issues and 'local' grievances with result that the charismatic element of the personality of a leader likes N.T. Ramarao of Andhra Pradesh, Laldenga of Mizoram, Subhash Ghishing of West Bengal and the like remains confined to the areas inhabited by the people of the same stock. An effort made by NTR to convert his Telugu Desam into Bharata Desam failed to make any headway.

It is a patent fact that the identity of a regional political party is marked by its area of operation, but in the case of some parties we may also take not of their eagerness to improve their image by establishing links with an all-India party either for the sake of bettering their electoral prospects or for having a mark of national recognition for instance, the Anna-DMK of M.G. Ramachandran and the National Conference of Dr Farooq Abdullah had an alliance with the Congress (I) and thereby they managed to remain in power safely. In 1989 the Telugu Desam, the DMK and the Assam Gan Parishad joined the National Front and subsequently became partners in its government of Janata Dal headed by V.P. Singh.

Important Regional Political Parties in India

Dravida Munnetra Kazhagam (DMK): In Tamil Nadu, the Congress maintained its hegemonic position in the 1952, 1957 and 1962 elections, by securing most of the Lok Sabha seats 31(41) of the state. Three general elections later, in 1967, the Congress was humbled once again, more decisively this time, by the Dravida Munnetra Kazhagam (DMK), a relatively young regional Political Party, which, however, has its origin in the Dravidian Movement which represented since the 1930s the Political, Social and Cultural aspirations of the ancient Tamil Community.

The Dravida Munnetra Kazhagam was launched in 1949 by C.N. Annadurai and his followers, who broke away from the Dravidar Kazhagam led by rationalist and socialist reformer E.V. Ramaswami Naiker.[42] In pre-independence India there used to be a party known as Justice Party in the then Madras province. Justice Party anti- Brahmin, anti-Congress, and Pro-British, it contested in 1937 election with the implied support of colonial masters but lost the Congress secured a grand victory. The Congress in Madras province was dominated by the Brahmins. The non-Brahmin castes organised themselves in this party. It gave way to another party known as Dravid Kazhagam led by E.V. Ramaswamy Naikar. Naikar was basically a social reformer and was opposed to the Brahminical hegemony over Hindu society. He fought for social justice and propagated his ideology among the non-Brahmin Communities. But his image was tarnished when he, in his seventies, married a girl of 28 years which was against the objectives of the party. The Kazhagam had demanded that the practice of unequal marriages should be banned. This antagonised his own followers.

Under these circumstances a new party, known as Dravida Munnetra Kazhagam (DMK), under the leadership of Annadurai took its shape. It was an anti-Brahmin Party. It propagated the legacy of Tamil culture and its emphasis was on Tamil history, literature and Tamil art. The main electoral base of the party was the middle class.[43]

The DMK got first success in 1959, when it gained control of Madras city-corporation with the help of independents from the Congress. In 1967, it became a ruling party in Madras with 138 seats out of 233 in the State Assembly. In Lok Sabha, it won 25 out of 39 seats allotted to Tamil Nadu. In 1971 elections, DMK won 184 out of 234 seats while in Lok Sabha also its performance was no less spectacular 23 out of 29 seats. However, in 1972 the party was splitted and M.G. Ramachandran (MGR) formed his Anna DMK. DMK lost power in 1997, which was only regained in 1989, when the DMK led alliance wrested 170 out of 232 seats in Tamil Nadu State Assembly election.[44]

After the ninth general elections in 1996, DMK became a constituent of the ruling alliance the United Front. In 1998 Lok Sabha elections DMK won five out of 39 seats from Tamil Nadu and one from Pondichery. It contested the 13th general elections as a constituent of the BJP-led National Democratic Alliances (NDA) and joined the government. It is also the ruling party (1996-2001) in Tamil Nadu.

AIADMK

AIADMK in Tamil Nadu is the breakaway group of the DMK. The DMK suffered a vertical split in 1972 when popular film star, politician of Tamil Nadu M.G. Ramachandran (better known as MGR) was expelled from the party following differences between him and party president M. Karunanidhi and his ministerial colleagues and launched the Anna Dravida Munnetra Kazhagam, (ADMK). The new party's leaders thought it wise to change its name by prefixing 'All India', leaving none in doubt about its stand on separation, when the Emergency (1975-77) was in force.[45] In 1977, as a result of agreement with Congress which gave more seats to AIADMK in State Assembly and less in Lok Sabha, AIADMK captured power in Tamil Nadu. In 1984, it got 12 seats for 18.4 per cent votes again in alliance with the

Congress. In 1987, there was a split in the party with the death of MGR. One group of AIADMK went with his wife Janaki Ramachandran while in other with his protégé co-star Jayalalitha. Both the factions contested the 1989 Assembly elections separately. The AIADMK lost the power to DMK in Tamil Nadu. However, both the group reunited after the defeat under the Jayalalita and the following 1989, Lok Sabha election saw the Congress AIADMK combine sweeping the poll. In 1991 state Assembly elections, AIADMK entered into alliance with Congress and the combine sweeped in the poll with AIADMK getting 163 seats and Congress 61 out of 234 seats Jayalalita was sworn in as the Chief Minister of Tamil Nadu.[46]

Jayalalita, an eminent film star, was also leader of AIADMK. She is a Brahmin and a non-Dravidian. The constitution of AIADMK is almost the same except that its members are not bound to profess agnosticism. The party aspires to be a national party.

In 1996 general elections, AIDMK was completely routed but in 1998 general election when the party had an alliance with the BJP, it won 18 seats. In 13th general election, which was necessitated because of Jayalalitha's decision to withdraw her support from the BJP and align her party with the Congress, the AIADMK could retain only 10 seats.

MDMK

The MDMK is yet another offshoot of the DMK. It came into being in May 1994 after V. Gopalswamy (now Vaiko), a senior leader and member of parliament, was expelled from the party in 1993. Barring, perhaps, their approach to issue such as 'Tamil Eelam', the Dravidian Parties do not have major ideological differences, particularly in respect of state autonomy, constitutional protection to the representation formula and making Tamil an official language of the Indian Union.

PMK

The Pattali Makkal Katchi (PMK) is of recent origin. Dr S. Ramadas launched the party in July-1989 by converting the Vanniyar Sangam he founded in 1980 into a political organisation. Its major planks include meaningful and effective reservation for people from the most backward classes (MBCs) and other socially oppressed sections such as Dalits and Tribal people. The Uinmiyar Sangam in the 1980s and the PMK in the decade that followed organised numerous agitation's in which thousands of people courted arrest and draved police repression to press the demand for greater social justice to the MBCs, the party's views on issues such as state autonomy, statutory safeguard for the reservation formula and the official language states for Tamil are identical to those of the three Dravidian Parties.

DMK, AIADMK, MDMK and PMK its role in Indian Politics

State and National Politics in Tamil Nadu have been dominated since 1967 by the two Dravidian Parties, like DMK and AIADMK. Both regional political parties started playing some role, howsoever small it might be, in the decision-making process at the centre from the beginning of the late 1960s, their actual participation in coalition governments came only in 1979, when two AIADMK members of parliament, Satyavani Muttu and Bala Pazhanoor, joined the short-lived Charan Singh Ministry which followed the Morarji Desai-led Janata Party Government (1977-79).[47] In 1977, the DMK allianed with the Congress, and the AIADMK allianed itself with the Janata Party.

In 1980, the situation was reversed as the AIADMK allianed with the Congress, and DMK with the Janata Party. The system of alliance and counter–alliance with the national parties thus continued. The DMK's Murasoli Maran joined the V.P. Singh Ministry in 1989. The DMK shared power with the subsequent United Front governments led by H.D. Deve Gowda and I.K. Gujral.[48]

In the post-1996 election scenario where no single party could secure an absolute majority in the 11th Lok Sabha, the DMK alongwith other regional political parties, became an important political force at the national level.[49]

The AIADMK went along with the Congress, while the DMK found its ally in Tamil Manila Congress, a breakaway group of the Congress. A majority of the Lok Sabha seats from Tamil Nadu, and majority of seats in the state assembly were won by

DMK – TMC combined. In 1998 Lok Sabha election the DMK stayed with the Janata Dal-led Third Front while the AIDMK went along with the BJP. In the Atal Bihari Vajpayee Ministry (1998-99), three regional political parties from Tamil Nadu, the AIADMK, the Marumalarchi Dravida Munnetra Kazhagam (MDMK); and Pattali Makkal Katchi (PMK), were represented. But AIADMK's presence lasted only a few months from Vajpayee Ministry (1998-99).

In the BJP-led National Democratic Alliance (NDA) Ministry headed by Vajpayee from 1999, the DMK, the MDMK, and PMK had their representatives. In fact, it was in this Ministry that Tamil Nadu had the largest representation. At one stage there were 10 Ministers from Tamil Nadu, seven of them from the regional parties.[50] For these four regional political parties, the DMK the AIDMK, the MDMK and the PMK in Tamil Nadu, the gains in the bargain are significant. Apart from strengthening their base in the state, it has helped them move closer to the corridors of power at the centre for what it is worth.

Listing the benefits accruing to the state from sharing power at the centre, the DMK stated that, "the presence of the DMK Minister (Murasoli Maran) in the national front cabinet and the resolution passed in the (Tamil Nadu) Assembly during the DMK regime (1996-2001) resulted in a Tribunal being appointed to adjudicate the Kaveri water dispute in the case filed by the Thanjavur farmers in the Supreme Court".

The real challenge for Dravidian Parties, however, relates to larger issues such as federalism, social justice, empowerment of women and Dalits and the language and cultural interests of Tamils, which the Dravidian movement has been espousing for long the association of the principal Dravidian Parties with coalition politics at the centre for over two decades has not helped.

Assam Gana Parishad (AGP)

Electoral Politics in Assam during the last one decade, beginning 1985, reflects the emergence of new trend. The one-party dominant system is giving way to a multi-party system in which political parties of various ethnic groups or smaller cultural communities play significant roles. The support base of the

Congress party shows a remarkable decline while a regional party – the Assam Gana Parishad, has been able to consolidate its hold in Assam politics. A number of smaller parties articulating the interests of smaller ethnic, communities, religious and linguistic minorities, have also been taking their presence felt. Electoral Politics in Assam is gradually reflecting the political significance of its multi-ethnic reality, with the respective educated elites of various communities consolidating their hold over the politics of their own communities.

Since 1952, except for the 1978 and 1985 assembly elections and its debacle in the 1996 election, the Congress has been winning all the parliamentary and assembly elections in the state.[51] But in 1977, parliament and 1978, Assembly elections in Assam the Congress Party share the votes very lowest.

The Assam Gana Parishad (AGP), was founded in October 1985, by a mighty student movement to protest against the influx of illegal immigrants from neighbouring countries across the border.[52] Two months after the signing of the Assam Accord (August 15, 1985) which brought to an end the six-year long, Assam agitation by the 'All Assam Students Union' (AASU) and an alliance of regional political parties and other 'non-political' structures under the name of All Assam Gana Sangram Parishad (AAGSP). The main demand of agitation was the expulsion of foreign national illegally staying in Assam.

Two months after signing the accord, the agitation leaders transformed themselves into a Political Party-the AGP. (Another two months later, the AGP won a decisive victory in the elections to the state Assembly and formed the first government by a regional party in Assam). According to the accord, the Assam Assembly elections were held in December 1985, by securing 67 seats in the 126 – members Assembly the AGP was catapulted into power just 67 days after its formation in October, 1985. Prafulla Kumar Mahanta, the leader of the AGP, became the Chief Minister of Assam,[53] wrested power from the Congress and formed the first government by regional party in Assam.

In the 1989, both the Telugu Desam Party and the Assam Gana Parishad (AGP) were in the National United Front of other non-communist opposition parties, with N.T. Rama Rao as its

Chairman. The more they would succeed in the National Front, the more they would be strengthened inside their states. And more successful they would be in solving their state problem, the more stabilised they would be in their states.[54]

In 1991, the Congress came back to power riding on the support provided by the Bengali speaking population, mainly the Muslims, who had felt harassed by the anti-foreigner drive inspired by AASU and sought to be implemented by the AGP government. The AGP aligned itself with the CPI (M) and the CPI for the 1996 Assembly and Lok Sabha elections. The alliance defeated both the Congress and the BJP, winning 70 of the 122 seats (AGP-59) and occupied the seats of power at the state level once again. At the national level, AGP was a constituent of the United Front, which occupied power at the centre during 1996-98. (This helped the AGP, according to one of its leaders, to become a "regional party with a national outlook". On way to this transition from opposition to the ruling party, from being limited to Assam to becoming a partner in the ruling combine at the centre, the AGP has had to modify its original Anti-Muslim stance and to become a representative of all sections of the population).

The exchange took place sometime during the late Hiteswar Saikia's second stint as Assam Chief Minister (1991-95). Responding to accusations that the leaders of the Assam Gana Parishad (AGP), the first regional party to have formed a government in the state, had spawned and had continued to have links with separatist and secessionist outfits like the United Liberation Front of Assam (ULFA), AGP Leader and former Chief Minister Prafulla Kumar Mahanta had said that, far being in bad with such elements, the AGP was in fact "a regional party with a national outlook". Never one to allow a political opponent to have the last word, Hiteshwar Saikia had countered by defining the Congress (I) in Assam as a "National Party with a regional outlook". On way to this transition from opposition to the ruling party, from being limited to Assam to becoming a partner in the ruling combines at the centre. The AGP has had to modify its original anti-Muslim stance, and to become a representative of all sections of the population.

In 1991 election the party had one MP in Lok Sabha, in 1996 there were five MPs but in 1998 and 1999 elections the party could not retain even a single seat. In 1996, when United Front Government was in power at the centre, AGP was a partner in the UF. The party is also in power in the state.[55]

Trinamool Congress

The year 2000 was significant in West Bengal politics because for the first time in 20 years a non-left board to charge of the Kolkata Municipal Corporation. It was first major electoral success of the newly born Trinamool Congress. Within a year when the state went to the Polls, the Trinamool Congress, under the Mamata Banerjee leadership, appeared to have attained the stature of a force threatening to unseat the Communist Party of India (Marxist)–led Left Front from power.[56]

West Bangal's left front (LF) government is a coalition arrangement with a difference. One party the Communist Party of India (M) maintains an absolute majority in coalition with a few acknowledged leftist political parties. Two Janata Party breakaway groups and the Communist Party of India (CPI) joined the left front in the early 1980s.[57] Trinamool Congress was the only party that looked like being capable of bringing about the change in government.

When the Congress, however came to be split on the question of the Congress leadership. The most popular leader, who was at one time the All India Youth Congress President and a Deputy Minister in the central government, Mamata Banerjee, was expelled from the party. She formed Trinamool Congress in January 1998, and entered into an understanding with the BJP. The TMC fought panchayat elections on May 28, 1998 independently. An unwritten understanding between the anti-left forces including the Congress and the BJP existed at the local level.[58]

The vote shares of the main left parties have remained almost unchanged, while the Congress vote was drastically reduced from 41 per cent in 1999. A large chunk of votes that previously went to the Congress was obtained by the new born Trinamool Congress with the 24 in 1998 and 25 per cent in 1999. This was major defeat for a national party like the Congress. Non-left voters reacted against Congress leadership in West Bangal, and particularly the younger one shifted their support to the Trinamool and its leader Mamata Banerjee.[59]

The Trinamool Congress Party entered into an alliance with BJP in the state, the alliance achieved a significant result in the 1998 parliamentary elections capturing seven seats. It conceded only one seat to the Congress and one to the BJP, which won its first seat.

Akali Dal

The Sironami Akali Dal was in existence even before independence. And it is both regional and communal party of Punjab. It emerged as a result of the Sikh's resolve to fight against the domination of British patronising Gurudwara Chief. In December 1920, the Gurudwara Reform Movement was invited to streamline the institutional set-up of the Gurudwaras, and to improve their functioning the Sironami Gurudwara Prabandhak Committee (SGPC) and Akali Dal were formed in 1924 as a result of the reform movement. While the SGPC with the passage of line became a democratically elected body entrusted with the task of controlling the Gurudwara, the Akali Dal became the political mouthpiece of the Punjab Sikhs.[60]

In the pre-independence days, when Muslim League demanded partition of the country on religious grounds the Akalis under the leadership of Master Tara Sing also wanted a separate Khalistan for Sikhs.[61]

In the 1952 elections the Akali Dal got 33 seats out of 186 member Assembly. In 1962 elections it secured 19 seats. In fourth general election of 1967 the Akali Dal maintained its position as the second largest party in the Assembly. The Congress could not get absolute majority, the opposition parties came together and formed a united front.[62]

In 1977, riding on the anti-Congress, pro-Janata wave, the Akali Dal came to power in the state. Once in power it started to pursue with the Union Government the demand of more powers to the state as contained in Anandpur Sahib Resolution was well as more specific demands regarding handing over of Chandigarh and Punjab and of more equitable sharing of Ravi-Beas water with its neighbouring states.

From 1982 onwards, increasing extremism and secessionist activities pervaded Punjab Politics in which an important role was played by Sikh religious organisations. The Akali Dal abdicated its political responsibility and surrendered to the extremists. Religions came to have total control over politics.[63]

In 1997 Punjab elections, the Akalis had an alliance with BJP, scored a thumping majority in Punjab assembly and won 78 seats. This was the ever highest score of the party in state politics. This was manifestly an alliance of both the Sikh and the Hindu Communalist.[64]

In 1996 General election it allianced itself with the Bahujan Samaj Party to win – 11 (Akali-8, BSP-3) out of 13 seats while the Congress won only 2. In 1998 General election their performance was quit impressive, and they joined the government. In 1999, 13th Lok Sabha elections, the Sironomi Akali Dal was allied with the BJP and won 8 and 2 seats respectively.[65] Today, the Akali Dal have a share in BJP coalitions government at the centre.

National Conference

National Conference of J&K is one of the dominant regional Political Party in Indian politics. It was founded in 1938, by the efforts of a valiant freedom fighter Shaikh Mohammad Abdullah, called Sher-I-Kashmir. With a modest beginning as a study circle in 1930s, it evolved into the All Jammu and Kashmir Muslim Conference in 1932. But Abdullah even at that time made it clear that, "the Kashmir movement is not communal but has come into existence to get the grievances of all the classes of people redressed". Under the influence of Jawaharlal Nehru, in June 1938 it changed its name and constitution to attract all sections and communities, and called itself All Jammu and Kashmir National Conference.[66]

Sheikh Mohammed Abdullah to do away with the government of Raj Hari Singh. His slogan was "New Kashmir". His party wanted the abolition of Zamindari, patronage to Kashmiri cottage industry and free education to women upto graduation. After Sheikh Abdullah's death, it is being headed by his son, Farooq Abdullah.[67]

National Conference is basically a secular party and therefore it has not deviated from its responsibility to encourage communal harmony. It was for this reason that inspite of the majority of Muslim Population, Kashmir took a decision to join the Indian Union rather than the Muslim theocratic State of Pakistan, unlike Akalis, Kashmir under centre.[68] Perhaps this explains the party's decision to support and join the BJP-Led Government at the centre in the 12th and 13th Lok Sabha elections. The party was represented by three MPs in the 12th Lok Sabha. In 1999, the party increased its tally to four. The ruling National Conference in Jammu and Kashmir State also joined the BJP-led Government in 1999 at the centre where it is represented by Forooq Abdullah's son, Omar Abdullah, as a State Minister for Commerce. Omar Abdullah, marketed as the their-apparent to the organisation built by his grandfather, Sheikh Mohammed Abdullah, was elected from Shrinagar.[69]

Shiv Sena

Shiv Sena, was formed in 1966 under the leadership of Bal Thakeray in the state of Maharastra. It draws inspiration from the great national hero, Shivaji. It wants to improve the conditions of the Maharashtrians in their own state. It seeks to free the people of Maharashtra from the injustice they suffer at the hands of big industrialists. It stands for the "son of the soil" slogan. Occasionally it resorted to violence to protect the interests of the Maharashtrians. For example, on the issue of border dispute-between Mysore and Maharashtra, the Shiv Sena tried to pressurizes the government in its favour by resorting to victory in the Municipal election of Bombay in 1968.[70]

By the early 1970s, the Sena had grown into a fairly strong Political Party. After winning the Municipal Corporation elections of 1968 and 1973, it began to set its sights on the State Assembly. Exploiting the crises in the State's Textile Mills during the 1970s, the Shiv Sena entrenched itself in a terrain that was once dominated by the left. The Sena candidate from Mumbai South Central, which is largely populated by mill workers and Maharashtrians with average incomes, has periodically won elections to both the Assembly and Parliament.[71]

Though Shiv Sena had been contesting elections, particularly at the Mumbai Muncipal Corporation level, for a long time its first success came in 1955 when it won 76 out of 170 seats in Mumbai Municipality. In the 1991 Lok Sabha election the Shiv Sena–BJP alliance won only nine, out of 48 seats it contested. But its electoral record showed a highly significant improvement into power at the state level removing the Congress which was enjoying power in Maharashtra uninterruptedly since 1960. The BJP-SS alliance won 138 out of 288 seats (BJP-65, SS-73), with the Congress winning 80. This improved showing was repeated in the 1996 General Elections when the BJP-SS alliance won 33 out of 48 Lok Sabha seats. It may be mentioned here that both in Maharashtra and at the all India level, there is an alliance between the BJP and the Shiv Sena. In 1998 Lok Sabha election, the Shiv Sena won six seats. While in 1999 General elections, of the 48 Lok Sabha seats in Maharastra, the Shiv Sena-BJP combine won 28 of which the Shiv Sena secured 15.

In fact, after its brief flirtation with a pro-Hindu, Pan-Indian ideology the Shiv Sena is now trying to rediscover its Marathi identity. A pure consideration of power happens to be the sole reason behind such a move. In 1999 Maharashtra assembly election the ruling Shiv Sena – BJP coalition was removed from power by a Post-Poll combination of National Congress Party and the Congress. Mutual recrimination between Shiv Sena and BJP followed this ouster from power.[72]

Today, Shiv Sena believed that it is the upholder of Hindutva. Infact, Bal Thackeray likes to call himself the "Hindu Hriday Samrat", the emperor of Hindu hearts. Over three decades the Shiv Sena has evolved into fundamentalist organisation whose leader never fails to use an opportunity to attack Minority Community particularly Muslims. Often calling them outsiders and threats of the nation, the Shiv Sean managed to party itself as a righteous vigilante organisation, always on the alert to protect Hindu interests. By playing the Hindutva Card whenever it can and regularly stirring up communal trouble in sensitive areas, the Shiv Sena has widened its net.[73]

Samajwadi Party

As indicated above Mulayam Singh Yadav was the first man to break away from Janata Dal and he founded a new party known as Samajwadi Party. This party has considerable influence in Uttar Pradesh and some pockets of Bihar and Maharashtra. Starting his political career as a Lohia socialist, Mulayam Singh Yadav raised the demand for raising the status of castes. He organised the members of this caste while ensuring that the party was not dubbed as a castist party. He, therefore, included some non-Yadavs also in the party.

BJP's movement for the construction of Ram Mandir at Ayodhya came to him as a blessing in disguise. As Chief Minister of Uttar Pradesh he took strict measures to fail the designs of "Karasevaks" to demolish the Babri Masjid.

Thus, Yadavs and Muslims became his strongest mass base. When United Front came to power in the eleventh Lok Sabha, Samajwadi Party became its partner and Mulayam Singh Yadav was its Defense Minister. It won 26 out of 151 seats it contested in the 13th general elections.

Samata Party

The other breakaway group from the parent organisation was Samata Party. It comprised mostly of Kurmis. Kurmis are better educated than Yadavs and therefore they had a better representation in government services. This created a sort of jealousy among Yadvas against Kurmis. Laloo Prasad Yadav was the acknowledged leader of the Yadav community and Nitish Kumar of the Kurmis. The two, although belonging to Lohia's party and product of JP movement, could not put up with each other for long. Hence there was a split.

Right from the united Janata Dal days George Fernandes had been contesting elections from Bihar. Although he belongs to Karnataka, he has no mass base there. After the emergency when the elections were held he fought election from a Bihar constituency. Inspite of his being in jail at that time, he won with a record margin. Thus, Bihar became his *Karmabhumi*. He was also dissatisfied with Laloo's arrogant behaviour and style of functioning. Therefore, he joined hands with Nitish Kumar and they together provided leadership to the new political formation.

This party is also ideology free. It claims to be the champion of social justice, stands for the uplift of the backwards. Yet, it has no hesitation in joining hands with the forces of *status-quo*, as is obvious from its alliance with BJP. The Samata Party, in its election manifesto issued on the eve of twelfth Lok Sabha elections expressed disagreement with BJP on issues like abrogation of Article 370, construction of Ram Mandir and Uniform Civil Code. Inspite of these differences, it did not mind fighting election in co-operation with it in 1999 and 1998. Both George and Nitish were ministers in BJP-led coalition at the centre.

It is manifest from the above that the only factor responsible for the emergence of Samata Party is anti-Lalooism by itself, it has a limited mass base and since the castes which support this party are not that numerous which Yadavas are, therefore, it can be concluded that its influence is concentrated only amongst the Kurmis and Coers. In 1996 elections it had an electoral alliance with BJP. This gave dividends to both the parties. Because of the influence of BJP amongst upper castes, it got the solid support of the people belonging to these communities. Outside Bihar it has some pockets of influence in Uttar Pradesh also.

It may thus be averred that inspite of its claim to be based on socialism, it is, in fact, a caste organisation. Instead of being a vehicle of social change, it has become a symbol of status-quoism.

Telugu Desam Party (TDP)

Telugu Desam Party was formed by the film star turned politician NTR. The party got a massive mandate in 1983 elections with 202 seats out of 294 seats. Not only did the TDP capture the majority of seats in the Assembly, but also had its representatives elected to the Lok Sabha and Rajya Sabha. In fact, in the Lok Sabha it emerged as the single largest opposition party in 1984, with more members than the other national parties.

Rashtriya Janata Dal

The personal ego between Sharad Yadav and Laloo Prasad Yadav brought about another split in Janata Dal. In 1997, Laloo Yadav formed his own political outfit known as Rashtriya Janata Dal (RJD). Since Laloo has a support base among members of his community, he remained a force to be reckoned with. His

RJD, therefore, became a real Janata Dal in Bihar and the rump was reduced to being the so called Janata Dal. The 1998 elections demonstrated that his mass base remained intact and Janata Dal became a non entity.

Laloo Prasad Yadav has his clout among Muslims also. It was he who had stopped Advani's *Rath Yatra*. Not only this, he put him behind the bars also. This earned for him a goodwill among Muslims and therefore as he himself says that he has the support of 'MY' which means Muslims and Yadavs.

Laloo is known in Indian politics for his gimmicks, especially for his rural style of speech. This has made him popular among the rural masses. It is significant to note that inspite of charges against him for involvement in fodder scam, his appeal to this clientele has not diminished.

Laloo, as he says, is committed to the cause of secularism. At least his unrelenting fight against BJP is sufficient to vindicate his claim. Prior to his breaking away from Janata Dal, he was one of its strongest pillar. One can easily conclude that the miserable performance of Janata Dal was mainly due to the fact that it had lost support of a person who could mobilise votes for it.

Like other off-shoots of Janata Dal, RJD also stands for social justice. Immediately after the formation of RJD a *Garib Rally* was organised by it to demonstrate its popular support. In this rally a slogan was raised saying *Adalati Nahi Samajik Nyay Chahiye* which means that people do not want legal justice they want social justice. This was indeed projected as a camouflage to overlook the charges labelled against Laloo in fodder scam. Laloo inspite of all the charges of corruption continues to have the mass support of his caste and social justice in India has become synonymous to reservation to the backward sections. RJD is committed to social justice. In fact, it has no separate ideology other than that of Janata Dal.

References

1. R.L. Gupta: *'Electoral Politics in India'*, Discovery Publication, New Delhi, 1985, p.1.

2. L. Muhinro Singh: '*Politics*', May-2004, p. 28.
3. Prabhat Datta: '*India's Democracy: New Challenges*', Kanishka Publishers, New Delhi, p. 67.
4. M.L. Ahuja: '*Hand Book of General Elections and Electoral Reforms*', 1952-1999, Mittal Publication, New Delhi, 2000, p.13.
5. *Politics* – May 2004, p. 30.
6. Ramashray Roy and Paul Wallace: '*Indian Politics and the 1998 Elections*', Sage Publication, New Delhi, 1999, p. 36.
7. Ramashray Roy: '*The Federal Experience India and Rassia*', Indian Council of Social Science Research, New Delhi, 2003, p. 50.
8. Babulal Fadia: '*State Politics in India*', Vol. I, Radiant Publication, New Delhi, 1984, p. 170.
9. Rakhahari Chatterji: '*Politics India*', South Assian Publication, New Delhi, 1999, pp. 51-52.
10. *Ibid.*
11. *The Hindu*, 7th November 1996.
12. *Economic and Political Weekly*, August 21-28, 1999, p. 247.
13. M.L. Ahuja: '*Electoral Politics and General Election in India*', Mittal Publication, New Delhi, 1952-1998.
14. Bhavan Mishra: '*Politics of the Opposition and Union State Relation*', Anmol Publication, 2000, pp. 66-67.
15. Ramashray Roy: *Op., Cit.*, p. 53.
16. Rama Reddy G. and N. Sharma: '*Regionalism in India: A Study of Telegram*', Concept Publication, New Delhi, 1979.
17. *Times of India*, 21st February, 1985.
18. Subhrat Datta: '*Political Science annual – 1996*', Deep and Deep Publication, New Delhi, 1996, p. 395.
19. Prof. Kalim Bahadur, MC Paul: '*Contemporary India*', Authors Press New Delhi, 2000, pp. 32-33.
20. *Third Concept* – April / May – 1998, p. 45.

21. Prof. Kalim Bahadur and Dr C.M. Paul: *Op., Cit.*, p. 34.

22. Ramashray Roy: *Op., Cit.*, p. 54.

23. Prof. Kalim Bahadur, C.M. Paul: *Op., Cit.*, p. 35.

24. *Third Concept*, August – 1998, p. 9.

25. *Competition Success Review*, May, 1999, p.15.

26. *Ibid.,* p. 19.

27. Prof. Kalim Bahadur and Dr M.C. Paul: *Op., Cit.*, p.133.

28. *Politics*, May, 2004, p. 28.

29. Sudhakar Kumar Singh: *'Regionalization of Indian Politics'*, *Third Concept,* October/November 1999, p. 31.

30. Ruchi Taygi: *'The Mandate of 2004 elections' Politics,* June-2004, p. 7.

31. *Frontline*, April 23rd 2004, p. 9.

32. V. Bhaskar Rao and B. Venkateshwaralu: *'Parliamentary Democracy in India'*, Mittal Publication, Delhi,1987, p.155.

33. Shriram Maheshwari: *'Political Development in India'*, Concept Publishing House, New Delhi, 1984, p.70.

34. Kalpan Rajaram: *'Indian Polity'*, Spectrum Book Pvt. Ltd., New Delhi, 2002, p. 363.

35. *Frontline,* April 23, 2004, p. 4.

36. V. Bhaskar Rao, B. Venkateshwaralu: *Op., Cit.*, p. 155.

37. A.K. Majumdar, Bhanwar Singh: *'Social life and socialism in India',* BRSA Publishers, Jaipur – 2000, p. 267.

38. Harinder, K. Chhabra, W.T. Jones: *'State Polities in India'*, Surjeet Publication, Delhi, 1980, p. 362.

39. R.L. Gupta, *Op., Cit.*, p. 19.

40. J.C. Johari: *'Indian Political System'*, Anmol Publication, New Delhi, 1995, p. 252.

41. Prof. Kalim, Bahadur, Dr M.C. Paul: *Op., Cit.*, pp. 33-34.

42. *Frontline*, April 23, 2004, p. 5.
43. M.L. Ahuja: *Op., Cit.*, p. 232.
44. S.S. Awasthy: '*Indian Government and Politics*', Har-Anand Publication, Delhi, 1999, p. 342.
45. *Frontline*, April 23, 2004, p.17.
46. S.S. Awasthy: *Op., Cit.*, p. 343.
47. *Frontline*, April 23, 2004, p.16.
48. Rakhahari Chatterji: *Op., Cit.*, p.78.
49. *Ibid.*
50. *Frontline*, April 23, 2004, p.16.
51. *Economic and Political Weakly* (EPW), August 21-28, 1999, p. 249.
52. M.L. Ahuja: *Op., Cit.*, p. 235.
53. Shiva Chandra Jha: '*Indian Party Politics*', Deep and Deep Publication, New Delhi, 1992.
54. *Ibid.*
55. Rakhahari Chatterji, *Op., Cit.*, p. 82.
56. Suhrid Shankar Chattopadyaya: '*Trinamool Congress Victim of Whims*', *Frontline*, April 2004, p. 24.
57. Paul Wallace and Ramashray Roy: '*India's 1999 Elections and 20th Century, Politics*', Sage Publication, New Delhi, 2003, p. 249.
58. *Ibid.*, p. 258.
59. *Ibid.*, p. 262.
60. Rakhahari Chatterji: *Op., Cit.*, p. 79.
61. M.L. Ahuja: *Op., Cit.*, p. 233.
62. Babulal Fadia: *Op., Cit.*, Vol. I, p. 296.
63. Rakhahari Chatterji: *Op., Cit.*, p. 80.
64. Sadan Chaturvedi: '*Political Parties*', B. R. Publishing, Delhi, 1999, Vol. 23, p. 112.

65. M.L. Ahuja: *Op., Cit.*, p. 234.
66. Rasheeduddin Khan: *'Democracy in India'*, Publication Team, New Delhi, 1995, p. 91.
67. M.L. Ahuja: *Op., Cit.*, p. 234.
68. Sadan Chaturvedi: *Opp., Cit.*, p. 114.
69. M.L. Ahuja: *Op., Cit.*, p. 234.
70. Babulal Fadia: *Op., Cit.*, Vol. I, pp. 300-301.
71. *Frontline*, April 2004, p.13.
72. Rakhahari Chatterji: *Op., Cit.*, p. 85.
73. *Frontline*, April, 2004, p.13.

5

Coalition Politics at the Centre

The chapter traces the evolution of coalition politics at the national level since 1977. Although coalition politics of any significance started with the Janata experiment a genuine coalition government could install itself in power at the Centre only with the United Front Government of 1996. This chapter analyses in detail the problems of Cabinet formation and Cabinet management under various coalitions from 1996 to the end of 2000.

The Janata Experiment

Coalition experiment at the Centre can be traced to the first non-Congress government led by the Janata Party (1977-80). The Janata party was the offspring of the continuous struggles made by the opposition parties to pull down the Congress from power. Frustrated by the authoritarianism of the Congress during the Emergency (1975-77), certain opposition parties and groups decided to fight the next general elections under a common banner and thus provide an alternative to the Congress. On the initiative given by Jayaprakash Narayan who provided moral leadership to Indian politics at the time, the Congress(O), the Jan Sangh, the Socialist party and the Bharatiya Lok Dal came together to undertake the challenge.

On 20 January 1977, the leaders of the above parties met in Delhi to chalk out their strategy for the elections. As the first step, this development was to have a tremendous impact on Indian politics. They decided to fight the Lok Sabha elections unitedly under one flag and with one programme. Morarji Desai who became leader of the party announced the decision to go to the polls under the name of the Janata Party. An executive committee was set-up to monitor the selection of candidates, drafting of the election manifesto and management of the party's election campaign. The Swatantra party became its constituent on 24 January, 1977.

It was at this time that Jagjivan Ram, H.N. Bahuguna, Nandini Satpathy and others resigned from the Congress party and announced the formation of the Congress For Democracy (CFD). This group joined the Janata party as an ally. The Janata and the CFD mobilised all anti-Emergency forces in the country and ensured the election of a non-Congress government for the first time at the Centre. Although lacking in resources and organisational machinery the Janata had leaders of rich political acumen, led by Jayaprakash Narayan who had the moral halo of a national leader almost of Nehruvian stature.

The general elections were held during March 1977, and the non-Congress opposition could sweep the polls. The sixth Lok Sabha gave surprise to the country by defeating the Congress as well as its leader Mrs Gandhi at the hosting.

The Janata party secured 271 and the CFD 28 seats respectively.[1] Among the Janata party constituents, the breakdown was as follows: Bharatiya Jan Sangh - 93, Bharatiya Lok Dal - 71; Congress(O) - 51; Socialists - 28; Chandrasekhar Group - 6 and others - 25. The formal Constitution of the Janata by merging the constituents took place only on 1st May, 1977, i.e. after the formation of the government, although the constituent groups were fighting the elections with a common symbol – the symbol of Haldhar – previously allotted to the Bharatiya Lok Dal (BLD).

The disparate nature of the Janata asserted itself when the party was faced with the task of electing its leader who was to take over the role of the Prime Minister. Jagjivan Ram of CFD, Charan Singh of BLD and Morarji Desai of Congress(O) were serious contenders for the post. When Morarji Desai was elected leader and was sworn in as Prime Minister on 24 March, 1977, the other two felt betrayed. And factionalism continued even after the formation of the government.

The decision of the Janata government to dissolve the nine Congress-ruled State governments and hold fresh elections aggravated the infighting. The distribution of tickets for State Assembly seats added fuel to the fire. Seven States - UP, Bihar, Rajasthan, MP, Orissa, Haryana and Himachal Pradesh - were won by the Janata party in the elections of June 1977, and the Chief Ministerships were shared by the two constituents the BJS and the BLD. The other constituents were disappointed. In the Assembly elections that followed in February 1978 in the States of Andhra Pradesh, Karnataka, Maharashtra, Assam and Meghalaya, the Congress party made an impressive victory in the first three States. This gave further occasion for bitter criticism of the party president Chandrasekhar by Charan Singh and Raj Narain. Charan Singh had in fact opposed the election of Chandrasekhar as president of the party.

After a few months reconciliation was reached in the party with the decision to have two Deputy Prime Ministers. Charan Singh and Jagjivan Ram were installed as Deputy Prime Ministers. However, Charan Singh's faction continued to be active within the party and was routed in the parliamentary party elections in May 1979.[2] All the six important posts in the parliamentary party were won by an informal alliance of the BJS and the Congress(O) groups. Charan Singh continued to entertain hopes about becoming the Prime Minister and Raj Narain, a socialist and Charan Singh's close associate, used every opportunity to press for the same. Although it was Raj Narain who was responsible for the Allahabad High Court judgment against Mrs Gandhi which eventually forced her to declare the Emergency, he was compelled to seek her help and advice to overthrow Morarji Desai.[3] Raj Narain was removed from the national executive of the party for one year for his personal attack on party leaders and open criticism of government policies. Protesting against the decision and alleging RSS domination in the party, he resigned from the party and formed the Janta (Secular). It was in these circumstances that the Congress party had brought a no-confidence motion against Morarji Ministry and got it passed. On 15 July, 1979 Morarji Desai submitted his resignation.[4] Following the Ministry's fall Charan Singh left the party and formed a separate Janata (J) party. Bahuguna, S.N. Misra and others also deserted the Janata party.

Y.B. Chavan, the leader of the Congress parliamentary party, was then called by President N. Sanjeeva Reddy to form the government. Being unable to secure a majority, the Congress declined the offer. The President then invited Charan Singh who felt confident of getting external support from the Congress. Charan Singh was asked to prove his majority in the House of the earliest possible opportunity within three weeks time. On 20 August, 1979, he submitted his resignation without even the confidence motion, having failed to ensure the support of the Congress. On 22 August, 1979 the President dissolved the Lok Sabha and ordered fresh elections. Charan Singh government continued as caretaker.

In the elections held in January 1980, to constitute the seventh Lok Sabha, the Congress (I) led by Mrs Gandhi occurred a two-third majority and the Janata constituents were reduced to small proportions. Thus the dream of providing a arable alternative government was shattered by the sudden collect of the party. The Janata was not able to attain the cohesion and unity required of a single party. The only uniting face was perhaps the nomenclature, the members being loyal to former groups to which they once belonged. The power-hungry Janta leaders were indulging in mutual bickering and mud shuging which made the government congenitally unstable. Lack of disciple among party leaders led to disobedience of the party high command and public criticism of governmental parties. Finally, there was no ideological homogeneity among the constituent parties which joined together to provide an alternative to the Congress(I).[5]

The Janata experiment came to a close with the disintegration of the party thereafter. It was either a single-party government nor a coalition government. Having had their experience and training in the single-party dominance system of the Congress, the leaders failed to imagine how to develop a consensus or coalition system among the different political groups that comprised the Janata. Eyeing each other with suspicion, the constituent parties forgot their competition with the Congress and indulged in conflict among themselves. Further their policy during the regime appeared to be remulative action against Mrs Gandhi rather than any positive programme of action to rectify the errors of the previous Congress governments.

The National Front Government

The next serious attempt to form a non-Congress government at the Centre was made in 1988 by parties called the National Front under the leadership of V.P. Singh, the Defence Minister in Rajiv Gandhi's Cabinet who had resigned in protest. The seven-party National Front formally launched on 17th September, 1988 consisted of a conglomeration of ideologically disparate, regionally based political parties and groups committed to ousting the Congress from power. The seven parties included: the Jan Morcha, the Janata party, the Lok Dal, the Congress (S), the Telugu Desam, the Dravida Munnetra Kazhagom and the Assam Gana Parishad. The new found unity was the result of the continuous efforts on the part of V.P. Singh and of N.T. Rama Rao, the Telugu Desam leader and Chief Minister of Andhra Pradesh.

V.P. Singh, after his resignation from the Rajiv Gandhi Cabinet and subsequent suspension from the Congress(I), carried on a campaign against corruption in high levels and formed the Jan Morcha as a forum to voice his views. The Jan Morcha was welcomed by other groups and politicians opposed to the Congress(I) who volunteered to share platforms with V.P. Singh and organise joint campaigns to root out corruption and tackle other pressing problems facing the people.[6] This sense of co-operation among the opposition parties led to the formation of a common national platform for the Jan Morcha, the Janata party, the Congress(S) and the Lok Dal(A) led by Ajit Singh. A joint statement issued at New Delhi by the group listed fourteen issues which might constitute the core of the strategy to give the country an alternative policy, a new social order and a better tomorrow.[7] The list included electoral reforms, decentralisation of political and economic power, elimination of corruption at all levels and a self-reliant economy with rural parity. Addressing a rally in Bangalore to mark five years of Janata rule in Karnataka, several non-Congress(I) Chief Ministers and opposition leaders affirmed the need for forming an effective anti-Congress(I) front. The rally was addressed by several opposition leaders including the Chief Ministers of Andhra Pradesh, Assam, Haryana, Karnataka and West Bengal.[8] A series of joint rallies and conferences culminated in the merger of Lok Dal(A) and Rashtriya Sanjay Manch into the Janata Party.[9] There were similar moves for bringing together other opposition parties at that time. The opposition moves got an impetus from the election of V.P. Singh from Allahabad Lok Sabha constituency in the by elections held in June 1988 with a margin of 110,000 votes. Further, this made V.P. Singh the undisputed leader of the opposition parties, relegating the claims of other aspirants like Chandrashekhar and Devi Lal into the background.

Efforts to merge like-minded parties such as the Janata, Lok Dal, Congress(S) and Jan Morcha continued without apparent success. The main hindrance appeared to be the personal jealousies and amibitions of the leaders of these parties. After much dilly dallying, the Janata party, Jan Morcha and the Devi Lal faction of Lok Dal merged and finally launched the Janata Dal on 11 October, 1988.[10] The Congress(S) and the Bahuguna faction of Lok Dal remained aloof. The birth of Janata Dal was acclaimed as a turning point in Indian politics as it promised a centrist, secular alternative to the Congress. The new party was recognised by the Speaker on the floor of the Lok Sabha in April 1989 and was also recognised as a national party by the Election Commission of India in October 1989. Nevertheless personal enmities remained between leaders like V.P. Singh, Chandrasekhar, Devi Lal, Bahuguna, Ajit Singh and others.[11]

Simultaneously, parallel moves were being made under the leadership of N.T. Rama Rao to forge unity in the opposition ranks. This resulted in the formation of the National Front on 17th September, 1988 about three weeks before the formation of the Janata Dal. That is to say, the formation of the National Front preceded the formation of the Janata Dal. Of the seven member parties of the National Front, the Janata, the Jan Morcha and the Lok Dal joined to form the Janata Dal; the other four parties preferred to retain their identity. Thus the number of National Front constituents was reduced to five: the Janata Dal, the Congress(S), the AGP, the DMK and the TDP. N.T. Rama Rao was made Chairman of the National Front.

The leaders of the Front turned to the right and left quarters for support. Rama Rao held discussions with Jyoti Basu while V.P. Singh and others shared platforms with the BJP. But the ideological difference between the CPI and CPI(M) groups on the one hand and the BJP on the other stood in the way of opposition unity moves in the first half of 1989 election year. The second half of the year witnessed a change in the attitude of the political parties. The opposition parties realised that the Congress (I) was at its weakest and their failure to grasp the situation would never be forgiven by the people. In June 1989, the BJP President L.K. Advani announced the party consensus on the question of seat adjustment with the Janata Dal and other constituents of the National Front in the Lok Sabha elections.[12] After two more days the national conference of RSP held in New Delhi decided to have electoral alliance with National Front to avoid division of votes.

On 17th October, 1989 the Election Commission announced the schedule of the ninth general elections to be held on 22 and 24th November, 1989 the election proclamation brought about the occasion for a rare display of unity among the opposition parties. Seat adjustment talks with the BJP and the left parties got under way. The Election Commission recognised eight political parties as national parties with reserved symbols for the coming Lok Sabha and Assembly elections.[13] They were: the Congress (I), Janata Dal, the Lok Dal(B), the Janata Party, the BJP, the CPI, the CPI(M) and the Congress(S).

In these circumstances the BJP softened its stand towards the Janata Dal and the National Front. The left parties too agreed to make seat adjustments with parties allied to the BJP. It was clear that the old reservations had to be shed under compulsion of real politics. It was publicly claimed that the Janata Dal had made no open alliance with either the BJP or the Communists; but in fact their State units were permitted to make electoral adjustments with both.[14]

In the ninth general election that followed, the Congress(I) won the largest number of seats but had no majority to form the government. The Congress (I) made it known that they had no intention to stake the claim for forming a government. So the opposition parties started their moves. The National Front presidium met in New Delhi and constituted a five-member committee to initiate talks with non-Congress(I) parties.[15] The members of the committee were: N.T. Rama Rao, V.P. Singh, Devi Lal, Ajit Singh and Arun Nehru. The committee members held discussions with representatives of BJP and the left parties. As a result, the CPI, CPI(M), RSP and the Forward Bloc decided to extend unconditional support from outside to the National Front to form a government.[16] The BJP also offered to give "general but critical support" to the National Front to run a minority government without participating in it.[17] Meanwhile, an attempt was made to explore the possibility of forming a government of "national reconciliation" by including all national political parties, but the idea was not acceptable to all parties and leaders.

Seats Won by Various Parties in the 1989 Lok Sabha Election

Congress (I)	197
Janata Dal	143
Bharatiya Janata Party	85
Janata Party	0
Lok Kranti Dal	0
Communist Party of India	12
Communist Party of India (Marxist)	33
ICSS	1
Telugu Desam Party	2
Dravida Munnetra Kazhagam	0
Other Major State parties	22
Others	22
Independents	12
Total	529

Source: Deccan Herald, June 20, 1990.

The Janata Dal parliamentary party meeting, presided over by Madhu Dandavate, elected V.P. Singh as its leader. Although V.P. Singh was popularly thought of as the Prime Ministerial candidate, Devi Lal and Chandrasekhar were strong aspirants and were trying every means to subvert the election of V.P. Singh as the parliamentary leader. It was by prolonged persuasion and pressure that the two leaders were made to accept the election of V.P. Singh as the leader. V.P. Singh proposed Devi Lal as the leader of the parliamentary party and Chandrasekhar seconded it. But Devi Lal declined and proposed the name of V.P. Singh, and Ajit Singh seconded the proposal. The drama gave tense moments as there was a general fear about Devi Lal's changing moods. Madhu Dandavate then declared V.P. Singh elected as the leader of Janata Dal parliamentary party. Chandrasekhar, however, expressed his reservation about the manner in which the election was conducted.[18] Then the National Front parliamentary party also elected V.P. Singh as its leader unanimously.[19]

The President of India, R. Venkataraman, invited Rajiv Gandhi to form the government following the principle of first invitation to the largest party. When he declined, having had no majority for his party and having no intention to seek support from other parties, Venkataraman turned to V.P. Singh, the leader of the second largest party, the Janata Dal. The President stipulated that V.P. Singh would have to "take a vote of confidence in the Lok Sabha within thirty days of his assuming office", which he did successfully with the help of the BJP and the Communists. The National Front was supposed to be a wider forum comprising five national and regional parties; but the Janata Dal alone had 143 members out of 146 of the National Front. Hence the National Front was not in fact a coalition, and the National Front government was a minority government led by the Janata Dal and supported by the BJP and the left parties without participating in the Government. Nor did the Front parties have a common minimum programme to unite themselves and the ideologically distant supporting parties. The Front leaders did not think of evolving any mechanism for the effective co-ordination and monitoring of the government, not to speak of nurturing a new political culture.

The natural and inherent differences in the National Front government came to surface within a short time of its formation. In August 1990, the V.P. Singh government, following its own electoral calculations, decided to implement the recommendations of the Mandal Commission report under which 52 per cent of the government jobs had to be reserved for the Scheduled Castes and Other Backward Castes. The government took the decision without consulting the supporting parties. The decision antagonized the BJP as such a move would adversely affect the electoral interests of the party. V.P. Singh's decision was highly unpopular among the urban upper caste and middle class Hindus who served as BJP's vote bank. Further the arrest of L.K. Adavani in Bihar, during the course of his Ayodhya-linked Ratha Yatra, by the Janata Dal government of the State gave impetus to BJP's decision to withdraw support to the National Front government. On withdrawal of support by the BJP, the President asked V.P. Singh to prove his majority in the Lok Sabha. The eleven month-old minority government of V.P. Singh was voted out of power on 7 November 1990 with passing of a no-confidence motion in the Lok Sabha with 346 votes against the Government and 142 in favour.

The threat to the National Front government came not merely from the external supporters, but also from within. The Janata Dal was not fully integrated in spite of the merger of the Janata party, Lok Dal and Jan Morcha. Factions of the Janata Dal and Lok Dal had remained separate, protesting against the policy of the official leadership. And the factions that merged (led by leaders like Chandrasekhar and Devi Lal were unhappy about the dominance of the Jan Morcha and its leader V.P. Singh. This unhappiness manifested itself when the Janata Dal broke up under their leaders into new political outfits.

After the fall of V.P. Singh government on 7th November, 1990, the Janata Dal was split by Chandrasekhar who with the support of 55 members formed the Janata Dal (Samajwadi). Chandrasekhar assumed the office of Prime Minister on 10 November, 1990 with the support of the Congress (I). This was another minority government, not a coalition, solely dependent on the outside support of the Congress and was bound to repeat the fate of the earlier minority government led by Charan Singh. President R. Venkataraman is reported to have enquired whether the Congress support would last for at least one year. Rajiv Gandhi replied: "Why one year? It could continue to the life of the Lok Sabha."[20] Differences occurred soon between the government and the Congress(I) on various issues relating to Punjab, Kashmir and Assam, the economy of the country, rising prices and the questing of permitting US planes to refuel in India.[21] Finally, came the allegation from the Congress(I) that its President Rajiv Gandhi's residence at 10 Janpath, New Delhi was being kept under the constant surveillance of Haryana intelligence men. The Congress(I) walk-out in the Lok Sabha on this issue led to adjournment of the House twice for want of quorum. The Congress party's decision to stay out from the House until adequate action was taken against all concerned forced Chandrasekhar to submit his resignation on 6 March, 1991 and advise the President to dissolve the Lok Sabha. The President of India, R. Venkataraman, dissolved the ninth Lok Sabha on 13th March, 1991 and ordered fresh elections. Chandrasekhar continued as caretaker Prime Minister.

In the next elections held in May-June 1991, the Congress(I) emerged as the largest single party with 224 seats, but without majority. Being the leader of the largest party, P.V. Narasimha Rao formed the government and surprisingly he could complete the five-year term.

The United Front Government

The eleventh Lok Sabha elected in April-May 1996 witnessed a severely fractured verdict with no one party or alliance being able to come anywhere near an absolute majority. It was a multi-cornered fight, the BJP alone being able to give the semblance of an alliance. The Congress fought it alone with perhaps some electoral adjustments at the State level. The National Front (NF) and Left Front (LF) parties could not reach any agreement about a third front as a viable alternative to the Congress and the BJP. Despite several rounds of talks, neither the NF nor the LF could agree on their allies or on a common programme. The main cause was the absence of any strong focal point or a leader who could bring them together. The greatest obstacles arose at the State level, particularly in UP, AP and Tamil Nadu where the State unit leaders could not agree to work with their rivals.[22]

The BJP emerged as the single largest party with 160 seats as against 139 seats won by the Congress (I). Atal Bihari Vajpayee was unanimously elected leader of the BJP parliamentary party.

A delegation led by L.K. Advani met the President of India to stake claim to form the next government.[23]

Meanwhile the Samata party national executive decided to give issue-based support to the BJP and requested the President to invite the BJP leader to form the government. The President Shanker Dayal Sharma invited Vajpayee on 15th May, 1996 to form the government and asked him to prove his majority on the floor of Lok Sabha by 31st May, 1996.

Seats Won by Various Parties in the 1996 Lok Sabha Election[24]

Total Seats – 543

BJP and Allies	*Congress and Allies*	*NF-LF and Others*
BJP - 160	Congress (I) - 139	Janta Dal - 45
Shiv Sena - 15		CPI (M) - 32
Samta - 8		FB - 12
Haryana Vikas -3		RSP - 5
186		SP - 17
		BSP - 11
		DMK - 17
		TMC - 20
		TDP - 16
		Akali Dal - 8
		AGP - 5
		AICC (T) - 5
		Others - 19
		215

At this time the National Front and the Left Front parties were working hard to forge unity among themselves to stake claim to form the government as well as to check the BJP from reaching power. The Congress(I) Working Committee also decided on 13th May, 1996 to ensure that the BJP would not be able to form the government.[25] In a pre-emptive strike, the NF-LF combine elected H.D. Deve Gowda, the Janata Dal Chief Minister of Karnataka on 13th, May, 1996 as their candidate for Premiership, and the election was communicated to the President. The election of Deve Gowda was made after a process of elimination, with V.P. Singh, Jyoti Basu and G.K. Moopanar declining to take the responsibility. Jyoti Basu was in fact willing to become the Prime Minister, but the party politbureau decided otherwise. Still it was uprising that the claims of better known politicians like Ramakrishna Hegde were ignored. The leaders who supported Gowda and signed the communication to the President were: H.S. Surjeet (CPI-M), Indrajit Gupta (CPI), Laloo Prasad Yadav (JD), M. Karunanidhi (DMK), G.K. Moopanar (TMC), Mulayam Singh Yadav (SP), Chandrababu Naidu (TDP), Durgada Boro (AGP), Madhav Rao Sindia (MVPC) and N.D. Tiwari (Cong-T).[26] Deve Gowda now formally requested the Congress(I) to extend their support to the Third Front in the formation of government. However, the President summoned Vajpayee on 15th May to the discomfiture of the Third Front who criticised the Presidential action as "hasty".

Thus, the first BJP Prime Minister was sworn in on 16 May, 1996 along with eleven Cabinet Ministers. But Vajpayee could not settle down to office as he had to muster enough support to keep up the Ministry. Nor could the Third Front leaders, they being committed to snatching away power from the BJP.

The NF-LF leaders now renamed the Third Front as the United Front (UF) and formally elected Deve Gowda the leader of the United Front parliamentary party. The United Front consisted of nine parties of the National Front (JD, TDP, DMK, TMC, AGP, SP, KCP, MPVC, Cong-T) and four Left Front parties (CPI-M, CPI, FB, RSP). Deve Gowda's name was proposed by the CPI(M) leader Somnath Chatterjee and seconded by leaders of all thirteen parties constituting the United Front. By this time it was clear that the BJP government's fate was sealed. Vajpayee formally moved the confidence motion on 27th May and after debate on 28th May, he announced his resignation without facing a vote on the floor of the Lok Sabha. The President accepted his resignation and asked him to continue until alternative arrangements were made.

Then the President invited Deve Gowda, the consensus leader of the United Front, to form the next government and prove his majority on the floor of the House. Gowda was sworn in on 1st June 1996 with 21 Ministers including 12 Cabinet Ministers. Another interesting development at this time was the hurried formation of a Federal Front within the United Front by regional parties-DMK, TMC, TDP and AGP on 31st May, the eve of the swearing in of the UF government. A brainchild of Chandrababu Naidu, the Chief Minister of Andhra Pradesh, the Federal Front with 58 MPs was supposed to function as a pressure group within the United Front. With the aim of planning a common strategy and joint action on issues common to States vis-à-vis the Centre, the Federal Front was designed to be an instrument of regional parties to assert themselves at the Centre. The United Front drafted a Common Minimum Programme agreed upon by all partners as a guide to action for the new government.

The United Front won the confidence vote on 12th June, 1996 with the support of the Congress(I). Narasimha Rao, the Congress(I) president, affirmed that the Congress would not allow the government "fall under any circumstances".[27] Thus a genuine coalition government consisting of thirteen parties committed to a common action programme, and proposed up by a larger party without participation, came to be established for the first time at the Centre.

Parties of the United Front

National Front			*Left Front*		
JD	-	45	CPI (M)	-	32
TDP	-	16	CPI	-	12
DMK	-	17	FB	-	3
TMC	-	20	RSP	-	5
SP	-	17			
AGP	-	5			
MPVC	-	2			
Kerala Cong.		1			
Cong. T.		4			
			Total	**-**	**179**

The Gowda Ministry could not complete one year, for Sitaram Kesri, the then Congress(I) President, handed over a letter to the President of India, Shanker Dayal Sharma on 30th March 1997 conveying the decision of the Congress(I) to withdraw support "with immediate effect" and demanding the resignation of Deve Gowda.[28] Congress President accused the government of trying to marginalise the Congress and not taking serious efforts to check communal, divisive and separatist forces in the country. The Congress Working Committee supported Kesri's decision and authorised him to take appropriate action "for staking claim to form the government". But many Congress leaders themselves were surprised at the sudden move of the Congress President. Although a number of charges had been listed in the letter addressed to the President of India, the real reason lay elsewhere.[29] The Gowda government had by this time decided to reopen investigation in the Tanwar murder case in which Sitaram Kesri was allegedly involved. There were also official moves to launch FERA violation cases against fifteen Congress Working Committee members as well as to question Sonia Gandhi in the Bofor investigation case. In these circumstances the Congress felt the need of having a friendly Prime Minister at the Centre. Deve Gowda, it was felt, was not friendly to the Congress President in spite of his being dependent on the latter and had spared no means to hit him hard or belittle him. The CPI(M) General Secretary Harkishen Singh Surjeet was dead opposed to any change of leadership and insisted that the UF alone would decide who the Prime Minister should be. So Sitaram Kesri wanted to form the government himself as Premier and hoped that he could get the support of some non-Left constituents of the United Front in the effort. He wrote to the President claiming himself to be able to form a government although the Congress had only 142 members in the Parliament.

All the Left parties in the United Front unilaterally rejected the idea of supporting a Congress-led government or of joining a coalition with Kesri as its head. As the possibility of getting the United Front support eluded, the Congress came down to accepting any other person as the United Front Prime Minister. But, Deve Gowda decided not to step down and was ready for a trial of strength on the floor of the House. The United Front needed 70 MPs more to survive once the Congress decided to withdraw support. After twelve hours of debate on 11th April, 1997, Deve Gowda lost the confidence motion and was asked by the President to continue until alternative arrangements were made.

Uncertainty prevailed in the political scene for a week owing to the firm stand of the Janata Dal and the Left Front against any change of leadership. The Congress(I) made it clear that they were prepared to offer support to the United Front if Deve Gowda was removed. Leaders of the Federal Front were, on the other hand, willing to make a compromise with a view to avoiding a mid-term poll. So a new leader had to be chosen who was likely to be acceptable to all Front partners as well as to the Congress. There were a few persons willing to be considered unlike on the previous occasion. The CPI(M) General Secretary successfully blocked the chances of leaders whom they did not like to see as Prime Minister.[30] Laloo Prasad Yadav, the Bihar Chief Minister and the Janata Dal President, was blocked on the ground that he was facing corruption charges on a big scale. Mulayam Singh Yadav, the Samajwadi Chief, was blocked because of recent embitterment between the SP and the CPI. G.K. Moopanar was disliked because of his friendly relations with Sonia Gandhi. The Marxists are reported to have apparently given two reasons for blocking him:

1. That the leader should come from the largest single party in the Front;

2. That the Prime Minister should come from the north Indian States this time to stall the progress of the BJP in the Hindi belt.

In spite of Moopanar being the front runner, neither DMK nor TDP came forward to propose his name. In the last stage Deve Gowda suggested S.R. Bommai, another leader from Karnataka, as he did not want Moopanar to emerge as his successor. Gujral turned out to be the final choice and his candidature was endorsed by the Front's Steering Committee. The CPI(M) did not project any candidate of their own, but put forward their criteria for selecting the Prime Minister. They also decided to keep away from the Ministry. Decks were cleared finally when the Congress submitted another letter to the President on 18th April, 1997 saying that the party would support the United Front Government if Deve Gowda was replaces by another leader of the alliance. So the gentlemanly and sophisticated politician and External Affairs Minister I.K. Gujral was elected as leader of the United Front on 19th April, 1997. Gujral was sworn in as Prime Minister on 21st April and he won the confidence vote in the Lok Sabha on 22nd April.

The fate of the Gujral Ministry came to be tested within six months when the Jain Commission report was submitted. A Commission had been appointed by the Central Government on 23rd August, 1991 under Justice Milap Chand Jain to enquire into the assassination of Rajiv Gandhi and find out if there was any conspiracy element behind it. The first report was submitted on 28th August, 1997 and placed on the Table of both Houses of Parliament on 20th November, 1997. The report pointed out that the LTTE was operating with the help of the DMK government and that the LTTE could not have killed Rajiv Gandhi without support and assistance from the DMK government and a section of DMK leaders.[31] The Congress President reacted immediately and asked the United Front government to drop the DMK Ministers. The Congress(I) was prepared for any talk with the Front only after the dismissal of the DMK Ministers.

In fact the Congress(I) was planning to overturn the Gujral Ministry by February next so as to avoid the presentation of a second budget by the United Front.[32] For they felt that a second budget would make the Congress weaker. The report had leaked out and the indictment of DMK was known before it was placed on the floor of the House. This was a heaven-sent opportunity for the Congress(I) who wanted to use it for creating a rift in the United Front, and they hoped to get the support of some constituents of the United Front.

Prime Minister Gujral rejected the demand of the Congress to dismiss the DMK Ministers and the whole United Front stood united on this issue. The Congress would have been contented with the "temporary removal" of the portfolio of Murasoli Maran, for it was a question of self-respect for the Congress not to support people who were allegedly involved in the murder of their leader.[33] But the DMK was strongly opposed to any compromise, and was encouraged to take a firm stand by the anti-Gujral lobby, in the UF led by the former Prime Minister Deve Gowda.

Meanwhile the Congress(I) again toyed with the idea of forming a government under their leadership, but none of the United Front partners was willing to join the Congress or tender support from outside. At last the Congress Working Committee decided on 28th November, 1997, to withdraw support to the Gujral Ministry with immediate effect. The decision was communicated to the President of India and on the same day, 28th November, 1997, the Gujral Ministry resigned. Although the majority of MP's belonging to all political parties were not inclined to face another election, there was no alternative. The President consulted constitutional experts and finally took the decision to dissolve the Lok Sabha and hold fresh elections. Gujral was asked to continue until alternative arrangements were made.

The First BJP-led Coalition, 1998

Coalition Formation

When the thirteen-day BJP government stepped out of office it had only three allies with it-the Samata party, the Shiv Sena and the Haryana Vikas party. Having failed to win over more members to keep itself in power, the BJP was convinced of the need to widen its net and win more allies to gain power. So in the 1998 elections it took the pragmatic approach of shelving the fundamentalist issues like the Mandir, Uniform Civil Code and Article 370, and thus made itself acceptable to other parties who had so far treated the BJP as unacceptable. They might have felt that the fundamentalist stance on Hindutva might not help them to expand beyond the Hindi belt. So the BJP strove to win over regional parties to get into new areas, particularly the south. It became imperative for the BJP to acknowledge the importance of the regional parties in their respective areas and align with them on their own terms. Although this was itself a matter of humiliation, the BJP could not dispense with it in the game of winning numbers. On the other hand, the regional parties with which the BJP decided to align this time were also at their loose ends, waiting for an opportunity to latch on to a national party to get into the Centre. AIADMK of Tamil Nadu and TDP (Parvathi) of Andhra Pradesh were under threat of extinction, having lost terribly in the preceding elections. Lok Shakti of Karnataka formed by Ramakrishna Hegde, Biju Janata Dal of Orissa led by Biju Patnaik and Trinamool Congress of West Bengal led by Mamata Banerjee were new in the arena and wanted to test their strength for the first time. The common interests brought the BJP and these regional parties together. Thus the BJP retained the relationship with the former allies Samata, Akali Dal, Shiv Sena and Haryana Vikas party and entered into new alliance with regional parties in Tamil Nadu, Orissa, Andhra Pradesh, Karnataka, West Bengal and Uttar Pradesh. The total came to sixteen and thus exceeded the constituents of the United Front.

BJP Alliance Statewise[34]

State		*Alliance party / parties*
Andhra Pradesh	:	Telugu Desam Party (Parvathi)
Bihar	:	Samata Party
Haryana	:	Haryana Vikas Party
Karnataka	:	Lok Shakti (R.K. Hegde)
Maharashtra	:	Shiv Sena
Orissa	:	Biju Janata Dal
Punjab	:	Akali Dal (Badal)
Tamil Nadu	:	AIDMK, MDMK, PMK, Tamil Nadu Rajiv Congress and Janata Party
Uttar Pradesh	:	Loktantrik Congress, Janatantrik BSP, Janata Dal (Rajaram)
West Bengal	:	Trinamool Congress

The United Front, on the other hand, consisting of thirteen parties while in power had lost its cohesion and failed to reach agreement on seat adjustment in UP, Bihar and Tamil Nadu.

Further differences persisted among constituents particularly on economic issues despite the release of a Common Minimum Programme and Joint Policy Declaration. The Left parties prepared a separate manifesto emphasising the differences with the Minimum Programme of the UF.[35] Moreover the UF failed to project a common leader or Prime Ministerial candidate.

The Congress(I) had entered into State-level adjustments with a few parties RJD, RPI, ML, KCM and RJP although it had not acknowledged the arrangement as a national alliance. The Congress felt a little rejuvenated on account of the "Sonia factor", with Sonia Gandhi having agreed to campaign for the party.

Election Results, 1998

The final tally in the 1998 elections came out to be as follows:

BJP and allies	251
United Front	96
Congress and allies	166
Others	22
Total	**535**

However, the sixteen constituents of the BJP-led alliance had been reduced to thirteen when the final results came. So the BJP had to accommodate only thirteen parties in the government they had to form. The seats were as given below:

BJP	178
AIADMK	18
Samata	12
BJD	9
SAD	8
Trinamool	7
Shiv Sena	6
Lok Shakti	3
PMK	4
MDMK	3
TRC	1

JP	1
HVP	1
TOTAL	**251**

Cabinet Formation

Unlike the 11th Lok Sabha where the United Front and the Congress together had 330 members, the 12th Lok Sabha witnessed an equal balancing between the ruling and opposition parties. Having failed to reach a majority, the BJP-led alliance could form only a minority government, and as such the question of its durability was in doubt. But the prospects of forging an anti-BJP combine was even less daunting. So evidently the chances of a BJP led government were brighter this time.

However, coalition management was going to be beset with problems. The BJP had to accommodate some of the most temperamental personalities of Indian politics. "Besides old friends like the temperamental Shiv Sena Chief Bal Thackerey and the volatile George Fernandes, the BJP will have to cope with the autocratic AIADMK Supremo J. Jayalalitha and the fire-brand Trinamul Congress leader Mamata Banerjee, not to mention. Subramanian Swamy who feels the Finance Minister's job is his rightful due".[36] Further as most of these new allies were in opposition in their respective States, their demands on the Centre threatened to multiply.

Such pulls and pressures had been in evidence no sooner than the election results were out. Jayalalitha who along with her four allies in Tamil Nadu commanded 27 MPs was giving the BJP sleepless nights even before Vajpayee was sworn in. She stunned the BJP as well as others by the announcement that she would extend only outside support to the Vajpayee government.[37] Then she made a retreat by saying that she was firm in her support to the BJP, but proved herself unreliable by the statement that she would take decisions in keeping the "the current situation". She was basically interested in overthrowing the DMK government in Tamil Nadu even if it involved unconstitutional means. Keeping such a person in good humour was perhaps the most demanding matter for the Prime Minister.

Equally problematic was the offer of "unconditional support" made by the Haryana Lok Dal Rashtriya (HLD-R) leader

Om Prakash Chautala despite the BJP's alliance with Haryana Vikas Party. Nobody was prepared to believe that Chautala was concerned about political stability and every body felt sure that he would demand his pound of flesh. Other regional leaders also had their regional sensitivities and personal ambitions.

Parleys started even before the results were completely out. BJP began informal discussions with friendly parties in its bid to achieve the magic figure of 272 members in the Lok Sabha. The Congress and the United Front also were making separate attempts to explore the possibilities on their part. The United Front was most strongly committed to forming a non-BJP government in the event of a hung Parliament.[38] The Congress President Sitaram Kesri appeared hopeful and held discussions with Sonia and other Congress leaders about the prospects particularly in the context of BJP's failure in gathering enough support.[39] Meanwhile the TDP decided not to extend support to the Congress, but sit in the opposition and tender "issue-based" support to the BJP-led government.[40] The TDP decision gave further confidence to the BJP although the AIADMK had purred cold water by the announcement not to join the Ministry. TDP preferred to remain neutral in the Lok Sabha where a confidence motion would be voted upon. Chances for a non-BJP government were finally sealed when RSP and Forward Bloc of the Left parties announced their decision not to support the Congress.

Since the Congress and the United Front were not making claims to form the government, it was easy for the President K.R. Narayanan to take a decision. He asked Vajpayee, who had been formally elected leader of the BJP Parliamentary party by this time, whether he would be "able and willing" to form a stable government. Vajpayee promised to present documents to back his claim of support from 262 members out of 539 members at the time. However, he was able to present letters of support of 240 members only when he met the President on 12th March, 1998.[41] This was so because of the last minute game played by AIADMK leader Jayalalitha who refused to give a letter of support in spite of her earlier pronouncements. To the contrary, she was reiterating her demand for the dismissal of DMK government in Tamil Nadu. She had other personal demands too. She wanted the Finance portfolio to be given to Subramanian Swamy and other 'plum posts' for her other men although she denied herself to have made such demands. According to reports, Jayalalitha had also hinted that the cases filed against her be withdrawn.[42]

The three-member MDMK, a partner of AIADMK in Tamil Nadu elections, who had intimated directly to the President of its support to BJP by fax now seemed to be retreating to remain with AIADMK. BJP had claimed the support of 228 of the prepoll partners including MDMK and 12 outsiders, i.e. 4 of Haryana Lok Dal-R, 2 of Arunachal Congress, 1 of Sikkim Democratic Front and independents including Maneka Gandhi, Buta Singh, Satnam Singh Kainth and one MP each from Mizoram and Manipur. The total number 240 was thus 22 down from 262 claimed by the BJP two days ealier.[43] If MDMK was to remain with AIADMK the number would come down further by three. Vajpayee and Advani again talked to Jayalalitha over phone, but failed to persuade her to tender the letter of support. Since the prospects of a BJP government was getting dimmer, the President invited the Congress and United Front leaders and discussed the political situation. Rekindled with hopes, they sought time to explore the alternative possibility. However, informal contacts had continued between the BJP leaders and Jayalalitha, and on 14th March she tendered a letter of "total and unconditional" support to the BJP and the letter was submitted to the President.

At this time there was a sort of a coup in the Congress, and the Congress Working Committee decided to replace Sitaram Kesri by Sonia Gandhi as President. Sonia informed the President of India of her party's decision not to stake claim to form a government. This smoothened the way for the President who invited Vajpayee on 15 March, 1998 to form the government and prove majority support on the floor of the House within ten days. In the numbers game that was to follow, the BJP and allies were to constitute 264 members out of 539. TDP with 12 members were to remain neutral and all others in the opposition numbered 263. This was a precarious margin of one vote's lead, but it was a decisive advantage for the BJP.[44]

Further parleys between Vajpayee's emissary Jaswant Singh and Jayalalitha at the latter's residence at Chennai brought her round to agree to join the government. Thus the AIADMK, PMK and TRC were to join the Ministry although Jayalalitha's plea for including Subramanian Swamy was not accepted. BJP leadership also agreed to incorporate the six-point charter of demands brought up by Jayalalitha in the National Agenda.

Once it was clear that Vajpayee had to form the government, he started confering with pre-poll allies about their nominees as Ministers and their preferences for portfolio.[45] There were already rumours about the names of important ministers and the allocation of important portfolios. It was generally accepted that Home would go to L.K. Advani, the BJP President and No. 2 man in government. Finance was a bone of contention; Vajpayee had his preference for Jaswant Singh who had been allotted the same portfolio in the 13-day Cabinet. Although he had been defeated this time, Vajpayee wanted to retain his services. But the BJP hard core did not like him. The party also preferred Murali Manohar Joshi to take the HRD Ministry. Allies had their own preferences, Jayalalitha having made them clear already. Akali Dal was interested in the Agriculture Ministry. An Akali MP who was also a member of the State Legislative Assembly refused to vacate his seat in the Assembly unless he got a Ministerial berth at the Centre.

Although the date of the Ministry's swearing in was fixed as 19th March, the list of Ministers and their portfolios could not be finalised even on 18th March. The last minute decision of George Fernandes to join the Ministry upset the pecking order carefully prepared by Vajpayee and Advani.[46] Thus Ministry making proved to be nightmarish to the BJP who had to balance the claims of the allies and those of the senior leaders within the party. Added to this was the request of Subramanian Swamy, who had been left out of the list, to Jayalalitha to permit him a "conscience vote" during the motion of confidence.[47]

Vajpayee took office on 19th March, 1998 along with a 42 member Council of Ministers, comprising 21 Cabinet rankers and 21 Ministers of State.[48] Of the 21 Cabinet members, 10 were from the BJP, nine from among the pre-poll allies and two Independents Ram Jethmalani and Buta Singh. Among the allies AIADMK and Samata got two Cabinet posts, and other allies

Akali Dal, Lok Shakti, Biju Janata Dal, Tamizhaka Rajiv Gandhi Congress and Shiv Sena – one Cabinet post each. Trinamul Congress did not join the Ministry and BJP's lone MP from West Bengal – Sikdar – could not be included owning the opposition from Mamata Banerjee. The notable absentee was Jaswant Singh who preferred to stay away owing to opposition from the 'Swadeshi Lobby' in the BJP. Among the 21 Ministers of State, there were 13 from BJP and eight from the allies.

Immediately after the swearing in of the Council of Ministers came the question of the election of the Lok Sabha Speaker. The BJP was inclined to taking the Speakership for itself and giving the Deputy Speakership to the Congress. But when the BJP floated the idea of evolving a consensus on the issue, the Congress-UF combine projected P.A. Sangma for Speaker. Standing on the verge of a confidence vote, the BJP was willing to concede the post to the opposition, and Vajpayee almost congratulated Sangma personally about his prospects. Suddenly, came the volute face on the part of TDP chief who hitherto had claimed to remain neutral on the speaker's election.[49] Thus there were two candidates in the fray P.A. Sangma of the Congress and G.M.C. Balayogi of TDP. BJP-led coalition was forced to accept Balayogi's candidature and elect him Speaker. After three days Vajpayees' confidence motion was put to vote and Vajpayee won by the positive vote of the TDP. The voting breakdown was as follows:[50]

Total strength including nominated	-	545
Elections to be held	-	4
Those who have not taken oath	-	2
Effective strength	-	539
Effective strength without Speaker	-	538
Ruling combine with TDP and 2 nominated	-	274
Congress and UF	-	261
Absent	-	1
Abstention (National Conference)	-	2

Coalition Management

Although the Ministry-making exercise was finished amicably, the Prime Minister's nerves were stretched time and again within a month.[51] First, it was the case of not including Jaswanth Singh in the Cabinet under pressure of the RSS. Second, it was the question of giving independent charge of revenue and banking to R.K. Kumar, a confidante of Jayalalitha. Third, it was the demand of AIADMK to dismiss the DMK government in Tamil Nadu. When the Opposition raised the issue of DMK government's dismissal in the Parliament, Vajpayee had to make it clear that the dismissal of DMK government under Article 356 was not a priority for the Government. But there was an equally strong demand from the Samata leaders for the application of Article 356 against the RJD government of Bihar.

Jayalalitha used to bring out personal enmities publicly and demand governmental action against persons whom she disliked. Once she demanded action against Sun TV which was owned by Murasoli Maran, a Cabinet Minister at the Centre and the nephew of DMK leader M. Karunanidhi. She had also demanded the resignation of three Cabinet Ministers - Ramakrishna Hegde, Ram Jethmalani and Buta Singh - with at least two of whom she had personal scores to settle.

Jayalalitha's obsession with DMK's ouster had led to raising the issue in a big way in the Lok Sabha and Rajya Sabha in June 1998. The immediate provocation for the same seems to be the order of a special court in Chennai to attach the properties of Jayalalitha and her confidante Sasikala Natarajan.[52]

Apart from the AIADMK there were other allies too who were unhappy about the situation. Resenting the big brother attitude of the BJP, some constituents led by the Samata party planned to form a pressure group within the coalition.[53] Leaders of Samata and Shiromani Akali Dal felt aggrieved that they were not being consulted on crucial issues like the Women's Reservation Bill and the creation of new States like Uttaranchal and Vananchal in which they had special interest. The Samata had demanded a sum of Rs. 50,000 crore for Bihar toward compensation if a separate Vananchal State was to be created.[54] Akalis threatened to withdraw support if Udham Singh Nagar was included in the proposed Uttaranchal State. AIADMK leader also welcomed the idea of a pressure group inside the coalition for her own reasons.[55] However, their efforts to rope in Biju Janata Dal and Haryana Vikas Party into the inner alliance did not succeed.

The general elections to the Legislative Assemblies of Delhi, Rajasthan, Madhya Pradesh and Mizoram scheduled to be held in the month of November 1998 occasioned a dispute over seat sharing between some of the coalition partners. Lok Shakti leader Ramakrishna Hegde wanted to put up candidates in the four States and had met the BJP President and other leaders in this connection. The response of the latter was rather cold and this left a bitter feeling with the Lok Shakti. Further the electoral debacle of the BJP in their traditionally strong areas in Madhya Pradesh, Rajasthan and Delhi invited criticism from the coalition partners themselves. AIADMK, the largest ally of the BJP, was the first to express a note of disgruntlement. According to Jayalalitha, the electoral defeat reflected a sense of popular anger and disenchantment with the BJP led government.[56] Trinamul Congress spokesman Ajit Panja spoke of the electoral verdict as reprimand for BJP's consistent record of neglect of its partners' interests.[57]

The Trinamul leader Mamata Banerjee, although not so aggressive as Jayalalitha of AIADMK, spared no occasion to criticize the BJP-led government of which it was an ally. She resigned from the Central Co-ordination Council to highlight the issue of spiraling prices of essential commodities although she continued to render support to the government. She did it with the hope of redeeming the image lost in the State politics at the time.[58] Their decision to observe December 6 as a black day to commemorate the demolition of Babri Masjid was an instance. Mamata joined the nation-wide protests against the attacks on Christians in Gujarat and Orissa. She demanded the resignation of Home Minister L.K. Advani for his failure to prevent the ghastly murder of the Australian missionary and his son in Orissa. She demanded the dismissal of the BJP Ministry in Gujarat for the failure to protect the minorities and of the Shiv Sena-BJP Ministry in Maharashtra on the cricket issue.[59]

The decision of the Central Government to effect a cut in food subsidy and increase the price of urea added one more issue for the acrimonious criticism of the allies.[60] Chandrababu Naidu, the TDP chief, called for the immediate withdrawal of price hike on food grains supplied from ration shops. Om Prakash Chautala, the INLD leader of Haryana, threatened to withdraw support to the Vajpayee government on this issue. AIADMK also joined the critics of the price hike and demanded a roll back. There was a general discontentment against the way the decision was taken without taking the allies consulting coalition partners is not morally right", they held.[61]

Within a few days the threat of the INLD became a reality when Chautala announced withdrawal of support to the BJP government.[62] But the government continued to take decisions without consulting the allies. The next instance of such a decision was the hike on telecom rates, announced on 9th March, 1999. The new rates which were to come into force on 1st April, 1999 had to be held back on account of a threat from Trinamul Congress to boycott the Lok Sabha session in protest.

AIADMK chief's relationship with the Prime Minister was getting strained on several counts. She was putting forth demands on the Prime Minister and the latter failed to meet all of them. Her demand for the removal of the Enforcement Directorate Chief, M.K. Bezbaruah was conceded, but her demand for replacing him by her own nominee could not be met.[63] Her demand for the replacement of Revenue Secretary N.K. Singh by the Banking Secretary, C.M. Vasudevan, was met half way. N.K. Singh was shifted to the Prime Minister's Office, but the post was filled by Javed Chaudhary. But her other major demands like dismissal of DMK government in Tamil Nadu, appointment of Subramanian Swamy as Finance Minister, etc. remained unfulfilled. She was becoming restive and more bitter day by day and went to the extent of indirectly accusing the Prime Minister of accepting bribes from a media baron who was being investigated into for alleged FERA violations.

No Prime Minister would bear such aggressive behaviour on the part of an ally. Vajpayee, as a countermove, wanted to drop the AIADMK ministers and even prevented Janaradanan,

AIADMK Minsiter, from proceeding on a foreign tour.[64] However, he was persuaded to hold his fire and wait to see Jayalalitha walking out.

The political scene in Tamil Nadu was changing. The MDMK leader "Vaiko" Gopalaswamy, an electoral ally of AIADMK, decided to extend unconditional support to the BJP government. And a few others of the AIADMK allies also showed willingness to join the government. DMK chief Karunanidhi, strong pillar of the UF, added a new dimension by stating that his party would support "all good schemes of the BJP".[65] He also added that all elected governments should be allowed to govern for five years. This indicated the possibility of a new political alignment at the Centre as well as in Tamil Nadu. The rift within the AIADMK alliance became so deep that the Pattali Makkal Katchi leader Ramdoss warned the BJP government against yielding to Jayalalitha's pressures and against divesting Minister Vazahappady Ramamurthy of the petroleum portfolio.[66]

The election of the Speaker and of the Deputy Speaker of Lok Sabha also added to the discontent. BJP's official stance that the Speakership should go to the ruling coalition and Deputy Speakership to the Opposition could not go smoothly. As regards Speakership, the BJP had its own candidate, but the last minute thrust made by Chandrababu Naidu in imposing a TDP candidate, G.M.C. Balayogi, shattered the hoped of BJP. However, Jayalalitha alleged that the BJP had agreed on the election of Balayogi of TDP without consulting the coalition partners, and so when the election of the Deputy Speaker came up Jayalalitha supported the Congress candidate in order to avoid BJP's appropriating the post for itself.[67]

The proposed Cabinet expansion announced by the Prime Minister on 12th January, 1999 had to be put on hold on account of the stiff stance taken by the allies. The Prime Minister, it was reported wanted to get half the posts for BJP and distribute the rest among the allies.[68] He entrusted George Fernandes with the task of contacting the allies and working out the arithmetic of representation. Jayalalitha seemed to have wanted to establish that she had the final authority to decide the representation from Tamil Nadu. She wanted four posts, besides stripping

Ramamurthy of the Petroleum Portfolio. Mamata Banerjee, insisting on the Railway portfolio, evaded any contact from the Prime Minister's Office.[69] The Akali chief informed the Prime Minister that the Akali nominee, P. Chandumajra, was no longer interested in joining the Cabinet. Samata Party was aggressive about retaining the Railway portfolio and further wanted two of their important leaders – Digvijay Singh and Abdul Gaffoor – to be accommodated.[70]

Within the BJP it was not all going smooth. The pulls and pressures within the party forced Vajpayee to shelve his plans for Cabinet expansion. There was demand for accommodating Sushama Swaraj as well as Sahib Singh Varma.[71] Problems were so intense that Vajpayee had to hold a day-long meeting with Advani and Thakre, two days before the expansion was scheduled, to discuss the pros and cons of effecting a Cabinet reshuffle at that time.[72] That made clear that Vajpayee did not have a free hand in Cabinet making even in relation to his own party. It was at about this time that Madan Lal Khurana, the Central Minister for Tourism and Parliamentary Affairs, was forced to submit his resignation owing to the hostility of the Sangh Parivar groups within the BJP.[73] The turmoil resulting from Khurana's rresignation reflected the growing conflict within the ruling party between a group of pragmatists who wanted to proceed with the job of governance and a group of ideologues who were uncompromising. It was widely held that Khurana's fall was manoeuvred by the RSS. Even when it was apparent that Sahib Singh Varma could not steer BJP to an electoral victory in Delhi, the RSS had resisted efforts to unseat him. Staunchly opposed to him, the RSS was eager to neutralize the 'Punjab lobby' that stood by Khurana.[74] Khurana's return as Chief Minister of Delhi would make him too powerful for the Sangh Parivar to tolerate. Since Kushabhau Thakre assumed charge as Party President, Khurana found himself at odds with the new dispensation.

The open fight had necessarily to be ended by an amicable settlement. So the leaders agreed to creating an institutional mechanism to ensure smooth party-government relationship as well as to avoid lapses in communication between them in future. The measures were to include[75]:

(i) The establishment of a programme monitoring unit and redressal grievance cell involving the Prime Minister's office and the party.

(ii) Daily interaction between Prime Minister's office and party office to ensure a common media policy.

(iii) Ministers to spare an hour each week for BJP workers and to appoint one party functionary in each Minister's office.

(iv) Holding daily meetings between Vajpayee and Advani, Thakre and Sudarshan, the Secretary of RSS.

(v) Ensuring that the different wings of the Sangh Parivar work broadly in tandem.

(vi) Projecting Vajpayee as a people's man.

(vii) Consultation with party and RSS on policy decisions and political appointments; and

(viii) Interaction between the party and its allies at the grassroots level.

The agreement was supposed to provide for a mutual check; but it was easier said than done.

The Sangh Parivar was trying to strangle the government by its dogmatic approach. The Vishwa Hindu Parishad's Dharma Sansad at Ahmedabad during 5 to 7 February, 1999 selected a revision on the fundamentalist question of constructing the Ram temple at Ayodhya.[76] One section seemed unhappy about jeopardizing the stability of the Central government over an issue that lost the political potential. The other group insisted that temple construction should be pursued to its logical end, considering the fact that a good portion of the work had been already completed. The consensus appeared to be in favour of deferring re-construction for two years. Yet, the dominant militant group in the VHP appealed to the BJP to hold on to the Hindutva agenda. The VHP also outlined a 40-point "Hindu" agenda, and announced plans to mobilise opinion and create a "Hindu vote bank" in order to free the BJP from its dependence on the allies.[77]

The party leadership minced no words in directing criticism against the government and its policies. The BJP President

Kushabhau Tahkre gave vent to his ire against the dilution of the Swadeshi plank in the proposed Insurance Regulatory Authority Bill and pointed that the government was not committed to its ideology.[78] But he was only voicing the anger of the RSS General Secretary and other hardcore men at the government's departure from ideology. However, ultimately Thakre had to come round and approve a Statement drafted by the Prime Minister's Office calling on all BJP members of Parliament to "fully back the IRA Bill when it is introduced and ensure its successful passage". The government, it was added, was the best judge of the need for such a bill.[79] The tension within the party made the Prime Minister fretful enough to describe the Indian democracy as "hollow" and party politics as "criminalised".[80]

Admiral Bhagwat's issue became another thorn on the Prime Minister's crown.[81] This gave a handle to the critics of the government to beat the Defence Minister and hit the Prime Minister. Jayalalitha demanded the resignation of the Defence Minister at the Co-ordination Committee meeting on 27th March, 1999, and referred to his mishandling of the issue as well as to the allegation that he was harbouring militants.[82] She also demanded that Admiral Bhagwat be taken back. But the Prime Minister ruled out any change in George Fernandes notion and rejected the demand for the reinstatement of Bhagwat as Naval Chief.[83]

Jayalalitha aggravated the situation by meeting Sonia Gandhi at a tea party arranged by Subramanian Swamy on 29th March. This was a part of the calculated move to undermine the BJP-led government with the help of the Congress. The presence of former Prime Ministers - Narasimha Rao, Deve Gowda and Chandrashekhar – at the tea party added political significance.[84] Immediately after, she put forth a three-point set of demands on the Bhagwat issue and declared that her party's continuance in the government would depend on the latter's response. The demand included the reinstatement of Bhagwat, the constitution of a Joint Political Committee to probe into his sacking as also the expulsion of Fernandes.[85] Although she said that she would give a reasonable time limit for the disposal of her demands by the Prime Minister, she indicated that she was willing to desert the BJP-led coalition and strike and alliance with the Congress. "If the government was a train", she said, "The AIADMK was the engine. BJP was only the driver. The AIADMK could push the driver out, and drive the train on its own. The train would go on even if some bogies dropped out. Even if all the bogies dropped out, the engine could go to the next railway station and attach itself to another train and move on."[86] However, the Cabinet rejected the demands of Jayalalitha, and that was enough to provoke her to withdraw her two Ministers – Thambi Durai and Janardhanan from the government.[87] The Prime Minister forwarded the resignation letters to the President, reportedly after asking Jayalalitha once more about the same. As the next move, Jayalalitha decided to step out of the Co-ordination Committee and started open manoeuvres to oust the BJP-led government.

The prospects of an alternative government were not clear. The CPI, CPI(M) and DMK denounced any combine that would include the AIADMK. But Jayalalitha carried on hectic activity by contacting MPs of various parties including the Republican Party of India, Indian Union Muslim Leagues, Kerala Congress (M), RJD and the National Conference. Laloo Prasad Yadav, the leader of RJD, announced with glee that the next Prime Minister would be elected within five minutes of the resignation of Vajpayee. But nobody could see any clear picture of the next Prime Minister, probably many had nurtured hopes about getting a chance. In this nebulous situation created by her own faux pax, Jayalalitha submitted to the President of India, on 14th April 1999, a letter withdrawing her party's support to the BJP-led government.[88]

The President advised the Prime Minister to seek a vote of confidence in the Lok Sabha. Although the President had not fixed any time limit, the Prime Minister decided to have the motion moved on 15th April. There were new political alignments. The DMK, the permanent rival of AIADMK in Tamil Nadu, declared support to Vajpayee. The INLD was won over to the BJP side. The Congress which was hitherto reluctant to provide leadership to the anti-government moves now come out in the open. The Left Front also worked hard to win some groups to the anti-BJP camp. Sonia could persuade the Tamil Manila

Congress leader to remain with them, despite their anti-Jayalalitha stance. The five-member Bahujan Samaj Party was decisive. Their last minute jump to the opposition sealed the fate of the government. H.S. Surjeet, Secretary-General of the CPI(M), was in touch with Kanshi Ram, the BSP leader. An early morning telephone talk between Sonia Gandhi and Ms. Mayavati made the difference.[89] Some individual MPs also had crossed the floor to join either side against the official stance of their party leadership. Saifudeen Soz of the National Conference and the Akali rebel Chandumajra had voted with the opposition against their party decision. Chaoba Singh of the Manipur State Congress crossed over and voted for the government. However, the BJP government lost the confidence motion by a margin of one vote – 269 in favour and 270 against.[90]

The Second BJP-led Coalition 1999

Having lost the confidence vote, the fate of the first BJP-led coalition Ministry was sealed. And the Ministry continued as care-taker until after the next general elections to the 13th Lok Sabha in September-October 1999. The electoral confrontation took place mainly between the BJP-led National Democratic Alliance on the one hand and the Congress(I) on the other, the third front failing to fructify as a united force. The NDA facing the 1999 elections was different in character from the BJP-led alliance of 1998 elections, with some of the allies replaced and the total strength rising to form a grand coalition of 24 parties. A pre-poll alliance electorally, the NDA lacked in the necessary cohesion and ideological and programmatic fusion or agreement that genuine coalitions were characterised to have. Some of the allies were conditionally aligned, like the Trinamul Congress, Telugu Desam and the Indian National Lok Dal, having their vital interests rooted in State politics.[91] The Biju Janata Dal and the Janata Dal(U) also had similarly strong regional interests underpinning their alliance with the BJP at the national level. The INLD, TDP and DMK were new entrants into the NDA, having left their earlier secular allies of the United Front under regional compulsions. With some of the State Governments facing Assembly elections - Andhra Pradesh, Karnataka, Nagaland, Meghalaya, Manipur and Mizoram - the national and State interests of the parties had to be co-ordinated.

The NDA's national agenda had to be mellowed down by sidelining core issues like the Ram Temple, the Uniform Civil Code and Article 370 in order to soften the non-saffron parties. Lok Shakti leader and Union Commerce Minister Ramakrishan Hegde threatened to walk out of the ruling coalition if the BJP revived its stand on these core issues. However, some of the partners like the TDP and Trinamul Congress remained outside the NDA's election manifesto and launched their own manifestos.[92] Thus there were contradictions within the NDA at the national level as well as at the State level. The NDA remained a loose and amorphous organisation without any clear control mechanism or norms of admission to membership. The Janata Dal (U) was admitted to the NDA on account of pressures exerted by Samata and Lok Shakti leaders in spite of objections raised by senior BJP leaders in Karnataka and Bihar. Further BJP did not consult the other partner of NDA when they decided to push out Haryana Vikas Congress and take in the INLD in its place.

The Congress (I) remained adamantly opposed to the idea of leading a coalition government at the Centre, and therefore there was no Congress-led alliance as such at the national level. There were a few electoral allies at the State level like the AIADMK in Tamil Nadu, RJD in Bihar and the traditional allies like the Muslim League and the Kerala Congress (M) in Kerala. Other anti-BJP parties like the Samajwadi Party and the BSP were equally anti-Congress(I) and were not inclined to have any electoral adjustment with either.

The election results cut down the representation of NDA's pre-poll partners in the Lok Sabha into fifteen, four of them having only one member each. The final election tally was as follows:

So the growth in BJP's strength in the Lok Sabha was marginal, having risen from 178 to 182, but the NDA's total strength was proportionately larger with a rise from 251 to 299. The National Conference, although not an ally of BJP in the elections, expressed willingness to join the NDA Ministry. But appeared to be deliberately non-committed about joining government, preferring to continue the policy of conditional and issue-based external support.[93] The situation manifested greater

Election Results, 1999

BJP & Allieas		*Cong. (I) & Allies*		*Left Parties*		*Other Parties*	
BJP	-182	Cong. (I)	-114	CPI	-4	BSP	- 14
BJD	-10	AIADMK	-10	CPI(M)	-33	SP	- 26
DMK	-12	KC (M)	-1	FB	-2	NC	- 4
HVC	-1	ML	-2	KC (J)	- 3	Ind. & others	- 21
INLD	-5	RJD	-7	RSP	-3	**Total**	**- 65**
JD(U)		RLD	**-2**	**Total**	**- 43**		
Loktantrik	-2	**Total**	**- 136**				
MDMK	-4						
MGRADMK	-1						
MSCP	-1						
PMK	-5						
SAD	-2						
SS	-15						
Trinamul	-8						
TDP	-29						
Ind. (Maneka)	-1						
Total	**- 299**						

power for the regional parties within the coalition, the DMK, TDP, Trinamul and JD(U) being able to be more assertive than the non-BJP groups of the previous regime. There were indications that Mamata Banerjee was preparing for hard bargaining in order to bag at least three major portfolios like the Railways and the Home and to put Ajit Panja, her party man and former Congress minister at the Centre, in the new Cabinet. The Sikkim Democratic Front and the Mizo National Front with one member each also joined the BJP coalition. Thus the BJP's coalition partners increased in number from 13 in the previous Lok Sabha to 18 in the present one, including Maneka Gandhi.

The President of India had no difficulty in identifying the party and the leader to form the new Ministry unlike on earlier occasions, and as such he summoned Vajpayee to hand the letter of appointment.[94] Vajpayee went about the task of Ministry formation confidently, consulting the leaders of allied parties and then entrusting Jaswant Singh to do the follow up. George Fernandes was given the responsibility of sorting out individual ambitions within the JD(U). Vajpayee was under pressure from his party headquarters to ensure that there was party representation from each State, including States that had no returned a single BJP member. The TDP stayed out and was contented with the continuance of the existing Speaker, G.M.C. Balayogi, a TDP member. The list of Ministers was discussed and approved by senior colleagues like Advani, Jaswant Singh and Kushabhau Thakre.[95] Vajpayee who initially planned to have a 50-member ministry of regions, coalition partners, experience, caste and other considerations.

The Third Ministry led by A.B. Vajpayee was sworn in on 13th October 1999. It consisted of 25 Cabinet Ministers, 7 Ministers of State with independent charge and 37 other Ministers of State, in addition to the Prime Minister, totaling seventy.[96] The BJP was in a stronger position in the Ministry, having secured 47 Ministers out of 70, than in the previous Ministry which had a 50:50 proportion.[97] However, there were disgruntled leaders in the alliance like Ramakrishna Hegde, Sikander Bakht and Sushama Swaraj who could not be included.[98] Some groups that joined the Ministry were not happy about the portfolios allotted to them.[99] Four of the 17 JD(U) Lok Sabha members from Bihar – Ram Vilas Paswan, Fernandes, Nitish Kumar and Sharad Yadav – were given Cabinet berths and another member, Digvijay Singh, was made a Minister of State. Yet there were unhappy MPs in the JD(U).[100] Bihar had the highest representation in the Ministry as a State, yet of no advantage to the BJP politically. Tamil Nadu was represented by eight ministers, three of whom were of Cabinet rank, two Ministers of State with independent charge and three Ministers of State. Still dissatisfaction lingered over the allotment of portfolios.[101] Inside the BJP camp, the RSS was keen that the Defence portfolio should go to a BJP leader, preferably Advani. But Vajpayee kept it for George Ferandes probably thinking that a transfer of Defence portfolio at this time, in the backdrop of India's victory in the Kargil war, would be interpreted differently. Both DMK and TDP liked to have Finance for their men, but Yaswant Sinha was the favoured choice supported by the business interests as well as by the RSS. As regards the Speakership of Lok Sabha, the coalition and the Opposition unanimously decided to give it once again to G.M.C. Balayogi, the sitting Speaker of the 12th Lok Sabha and an MP of the TDP. The Deputy Speakership was given to P.M. Sayeed, the sitting Deputy Speaker and member of the Congress(I) under pressure of allies, particularly of the Trinamul Congress although the BJP had cherished hopes about getting the post for itself.[102]

The first year of governance passed without much turbulence, although not without occasional turmoils. Differences of opinion had cropped up between the coalition partners on national issues like increase in the price of petroleum products[103], revival of Ayodhya issue by the Sangh Parivar[104] and attack on Christian missionaries by the militant communal elements. A statement made by Vajpayee that the demand for the construction of a temple at Ayodhya was an expression of national sentiments was vehemently criticised by the coalition partners like DMK. TDP and Trinamool as well as by the Opposition parties. It was even doubted that Vajpayee was favourable to the "hidden agenda" of the BJP and of the Sangh Parivar, and was appealing to the Hindu voters of UP in the context of the forthcoming elections of April 2001.[105] The regional parties in the coalition, particularly the Trinamul Congress, DMK and TDP had always been constrained by their State based interests and their political vision shortened by the State Assembly elections. Mamata's histrionies played in the wake of a hike in petrol and LPG prices and her threatened withdrawal from the cabinet on the basis of this issue were meant to humour the electorate of West Bengal.[106] Her continued demand for the dismissal of the Marxist led government of West Bengal, in spite of the Centre's rejection of the proposition to apply Article 356 in West Bengal, was a part of the poll-oriented political tactics.[107] Despite this kind of political games played by the coalition partners to strengthen their bargaining position within the Ministry and by the Sangh Parivar to have developed a consensus among them to pull on together. The exit of Pattali Makkul Katchi from the coalition and the resignation of its two Ministers in February 2001 were occasioned by regional considerations alone, as the party thought it advisable to latch on to the AIADMK in the State Assembly elections of April-May 2001.[108] The MK had no disagreement with the BJP; nor was its exit from the BJP camp meant to shaken the Ministry. But the PMK preferred to shift its alliance to the AIADMK camp on more pragmatic considerations of favourable payoffs in the State Assembly election than of any ideological or emotional reasons.

Co-ordination Council at the Centre

The concept of a Co-ordination Council to ensure the smooth co-operation of coalition allies was accepted rather late at the Centre. The United Front governments under Deve Gowda and I.K. Gujral failed to institute a common forum for the coalition. There was a steering committee exclusively for the UF partners and the proposal for a Co-ordination Council including the Congress did not materialise. The Congress President was not willing to be controlled by a Co-ordinating body as he was eager to have an opportunity to withdraw support.

While Gujral was elected Parliamentary leader of the UF, his appointment as Prime Minister was not all smooth. The President insisted on the creation of a formal arrangement for co-ordination with the supporting party. In fact Gujral was invited to form the government only after he agreed, in a joint letter with the Congress President Sitaram Kesri, to set up a mechanism of co-ordination consisting of five members each from the Congress and the UF.[109] However, the credit for installing such a council went to the BJP government. Some partners like the Trinamul Congress had initially proposed the creation of a Co-odination Committee, but its creation was delayed owing to lack of interest on the part of some other partners. It was widely known that the AIADMK leader Jayalalitha had preferred to be free of any such control mechanism.

The Co-ordination Council was, however set up by the Prime Minister on 21st April, 1998 to manage his temperamental 18-party allies.[110] It was to consist of five representatives of the BJP including the Chairman, and thirteen representatives of the other partners.[111] There was to be no rigidity regarding membership, as more representatives could be specially invited to attend meetings. Initially only the electoral allies were included, and the Premier was given power to decide if post-election allies were to be included, Vajpayee, the Prime Minister, was to be the Chairman and Jaswant Singh was made convener. Although the creation of the Co-ordination Council had been decided by the BJP and the allies in early March 1998, the matter was not given priority.[112] The first meeting of the Council was held on 9th May 1998 and it came off "successfully" in the thick of bargaining without sensitive issues being raised or thrashed out.[113] At least some quarters started thinking about strengthening the co-ordination process by holding frequent meetings of the forum and deliberating on major issues before policy announcements were made.[114] Suggestions like making the participation of constituents mandatory and ensuring the presence of a deputy to represent the group in the absence of the leader also came up.

Needless to say that no sincere efforts were made by the constituents including the BJP to make the Co-ordination Council an effective body. The BJP leaders often talked about "Coalition dharma", but refused to practise what they preached.[115] The allies complained that they were not being consulted on major issues and that the Co-ordination Council meetings were held only to get decisions rubber-stamped.

Trinamul Congress which did not join the ministry was unwilling to join the Co-ordination Council also initially. Although they joined the Council later on they spared no chance to criticize the government and in protest against some of the policies they withdrew membership of the body. AIADMK leader Jayalalitha also withdrew membership before resigning from the cabinet.

Thus the Co-ordination Council could not be made use of as a forum for effective co-ordination of allies during the first BJP-led coalition government. It became an object of contempt for the coalition partners, some of whom had not even liked to remain its members. Its status could not be improved during the second coalition too.

Personality Factor

There were three Prime Ministers in two years (1996-98); each one was unique in his own way. Deve Gowda was chosen as the Prime Ministerial candidate through a process of elimination and being comparatively unknown outside Karnataka. He was a dark horse that emerged on the national scene. Coming from a middle class agricultural background, he had risen to the Chief Ministership of Karnataka under the banner of the Janata Dal, the largest party in the United Front. With no command of Hindi and with a little of English, he tried to manage a vast country and an alliance of thirteen parties. Although dependent on the Congress support for his position, he showed scant respect for the Congress President Sitaram Kesri and often he tried to ignore him. It was his style of dealing with the Congress President and his violation of Congress interests that led to the withdrawal of Congress support and to his own ignominious exit.

I.K. Gujral, generally described as a suave and refined gentlemanly politician, was neither hostile to the Congress nor authoritarian with the partners. But the ambitious Congress President, in his anxiety to protect the image of his party in the context of the Jain Commission report, wanted to try his chances once more. Both United Front Prime Ministers were dependent on outside support and had difficulty in managing the Congress more than the coalition partners.

Vajpayee was in a more strange company than the UF Prime Ministers were. Some of the allies who wanted to show themselves as superior to the Prime Minister brought in 'ego problems'.

Some had ulterior motives in joining or supporting the government and sometimes made open efforts to promote them. He hardcore of his own party were never indulgent towards his policy of compromise. The task of knitting these divergent strands into a cohesive unit and providing a semblance of collective responsibility demanded a Herculean effort. Gupta and Bhaumik seemed to predict: "An easy going leader, Vajpayee is not known for either cunning or ruthlessness. He is most comfortable in mass politics, but the problems of coalitions are not resolved through thundering speeches nor is the party of much help. Most BJP leaders are inward looking and used to RSS inspired orderliness. They are usually at sea in dealing with people from a different political milieu. For governing with a wafer-thin majority, Vajpayee will need all the wily ingenuity of Bhairon Singh Sekhawat". Wily though he is not, he has had to use political gimmicks like one-day fasting to sideline his opponents and win public sympathy.

He could accept a high degree of self-effacement to keep the coalition working. Being moderate in views and tolerant to minority groups, he was the one BJP leader most acceptable to the allies. But the personal ambition and the private manoeuvres of allies like J. Jayalalitha, Mamata Banerjee and Chandrababu Naidu kept him on tenterhooks all the time. Even Manmohan Singh's UPA-I and UPA-II Coalition experiments at the Centre thus proved that the personality of leaders was an important factor contributing to the maintenance of coalitions.

References

1. R. Rajeeva: *'The Role of National Opposition in India 1984-89'*, Ph.D. Thesis submitted to the University of Kerala, 1997, p.108.

2. Indian Express, New Delhi, 17thMay 1979.

3. Arun Gandhi: *'Morarji Papers'*, New Delhi, 1983, p. 226.

4. Indian Express, New Delhi, 16th July, 1979.

5. R. Rajeevan, *Op.cit.*, p.113.

6. *Hindustan Times*, New Delhi, 28th October, 1987.

7. *Ibid.*, 29th Nov. 1987.

8. *Free Press Journal*, Bombay, 11th Jan. 1988.
9. R. Rajeevan, *Op.cit.*, pp.164-65.
10. *Hindustan Times*, New Delhi, 12th October 1988.
11. R. Rajeevan, *Op.cit.*, pp. 173.
12. *Indian Express*, New Delhi, 10th June 1989.
13. *Statesman,* New Delhi, 23rd October 1989.
14. Amalendu Das Gupta: *'Reversal of Roles, Opposition Loses Initiative'*, Statesman, New Delhi, 20th May 1989.
15. *The Hindu*, Madras, 29th November 1989.
16. *The Telegraph*, Calcutta, 29th November, 1989.
17. *The Times of India*, New Delhi, 20th November 1989.
18. *Indian Express,* New Delhi, 2nd December 1989.
19. *The Hindu,* Madras, 2nd December 1989.
20. *Ibid.,* Thiruvanathapuram, 9th October 1999.
21. Meenu Roy: *'Elections 1998'*, NPH, Jaipur, 1999, p.1.
22. *The Statesman*, New Delhi, 18th February, 1996.
23. Lok Sabha Secretariat: *'Diary of Political Events'*, New Delhi, Vol. 23, January – December 1996.
24. Subhash C. Kashyap (ed.): *'Coalition Government and Politics in India',* New Delhi, 1997, p.70.
25. Lok Sabha Secretariat: *Op.cit.*
26. *Ibid.*
27. *Ibid.*
28. Meenu Roy: *Op.cit.,* p. 4.
29. *Ibid.,* p. 5.
30. *'Politics India',* Vol. 1, No. 12, June 1997. p. 44.
31. Meenu Roy: *Op.cit.*

32. *'Politics India'*, Vol. II, No. 4, October 1997, p. 46.
33. Meenu Roy, *Op.cit.*, p. 9.
34. *Ibid.*, p. 179.
35. *The Hindu,* Thiruvananthapuram, 2nd February 1998.
36. Swapan Das Gupta and Saba Naqui Bhaumik: *'Crown of Thoms'*, India Today, 16th March 1998, p. 14.
37. *Ibid.*, p. 15.
38. *The Hindu*, Thiruvananthapuram, 2nd March 1998.
39. *Ibid.*, 4th March 1998.
40. *Ibid.*, 5th March 1998.
41. *Ibid.*, 13th March 1998.
42. *Ibid.*
43. *Ibid.*
44. *Ibid.*, 16th March 1998.
45. The Hindu, 17th March 1998.
46. *The Hindu*, 19th March 1998.
47. *Ibid.*
48. *The Hindu,* 20th March 1998.
49. *The Hindu,* Thiruvananthapuram, 22nd March 1998.
50. *Ibid.,* 25th March 1998.
51. *Ibid.*, 20th April 1998.
52. *Telegraph*, 6th June 1998.
53. *The Pioneer*, 16th July, 1998.
54. Suman K. Jha: *'Sordid Politics of Coalition'*, The Pioneer, 21st August 1998.
55. *Op.cit.*
56. Sukumar Muraleedharan: *'A Debacle in Nine Months'*, Frontline, 18th December 1998, p. 5.

57. *Ibid.*
58. *The Hindu*, Thiruvananthapuram, 4th November 1998.
59. Bal Thackeray, 'The Shiva Sena Chief' had announced that he would block the Pakistani cricket team visiting India. This had raised a furore all over the country.
60. *The Hindu*, Thiruvananthapuram, 30th June 1999.
61. *Ibid.,* 2nd February 1999.
62. *Ibid.,* 17th February 1999.
63. Indian Today, *"Life After...."*; 31st August 1998, pp.19–20.
64. *Ibid.*
65. *Ibid.*
66. *Indian Express,* Kochi, 13th October 1998.
67. *The Hindu*, Thiruvananthapuram, 10th December 1998.
68. *Ibid.*, 3rd January 1999.
69. It may be remembered that the Trinamool Congress led by Mamata Banerjee had not so far joined the government.
70. *The Hindu,* Thiruvananthapuram, 14th January 1999.
71. Earlier Sushma Swaraj was a Cabinet Minister at the Centre and Sahib Singh Varma the Chief Minister of Delhi. When the Delhi Assembly election came BJP high command removed Varma from the Chief Ministership and put Sushma there, thinking that she would be able to recover the image of the party. But the party lost majority and Sushma also lost the election. Thus both Sushma and Varma waited to be placed in the central Cabinet.
72. *The Hindu,* Thiruvananthapuram, 24th January 1999.
73. *The Hindu*, 31st January 1999.
74. V. Venkatesan: *'The War Within'*, Frontline, 26th February 1999, p.17.
75. Prabhu Chawla: *'Ready to Battle'*, India Today, 21st December 1998, p. 22.

76. Sukumar Muraleedharan: *'Disintegrating Coalition'*, Frontline, 26th February 1999, p. 8.

77. V. Venkatesan: *Op.cit.*, p. 20.

78. Prabhu Chawla, *Op.cit.*, p. 20.

79. *Ibid.*

80. Praful Bidwai: *"Hindutva and moth-eaten governance"*, Frontline, 26th February 1999, p.16.

81. Admiral Vishnu Bhagwat was Chief of Naval Staff when he was dismissed by the BJP government on alleged security reasons. The dismissal became controversial as it provoked criticism among the service staff as well as politicians. Bhagwat sought to move the court against the dismissal. However the government stood firm in the decision and did not reinstate Bhagwat.

82. *The Hindu,* Thiruvananthapuram, 28th March 1999.

83. *Ibid.,* 30th March 1999.

84. *Ibid.,* 30th March 1999.

85. *Ibid.,* 1st April 1999.

86. *Ibid.*

87. *Ibid.,* 6th April1999.

88. *Hindustan Times,* 15th April 1999.

89. *Ibid.,* 18th April 1999.

90. *Ibid.*

91. Sukumar Muraleedharan: *'The Unaligned Players'*, Frontline, 24th September 1999, p. 10.

92. V. Venkatesan: *'Coalition Constraints'*, Frontline, 21st September 1999, p.20.

93. *The Hindu,* Thiruvananthapuram, 8th October, 1999.

94. *Ibid.*, 12th October,1999.

95. *Ibid.*, 13th October, 1999.

96. *Ibid.,* 14th October, 1999.

97. V. Venkatesan: *'A Balancing Act'*, Frontline, 19th November 1999, p.24.

98. Ramakrishna Hegde's inclusion was opposed by the BJP unit of Karnataka which had not taken kindly in Hegde's role in pushing the JD(U) into the NDA, Hegde's strategy was blamed as the cause for the miserable failure of NDA and the JD(U) in the elections to the Kanataka Assembly as well as to the Lok Sabha. This was consequent of the split of Janata Dal into JD (United) and JD (Secular) when a group led by Sharad Yadav, President of JD decided to merge with Lok Shakti and Samata Party. However the merger of the three groups did not materialise although the split of the JD remained so. Sikander Bakht, the only Muslim Minister in the previous Ministry, was dropped. Barnala was expected to represent Akali Dal in the new Ministry, but he could not win the elections. The other Akali MP, Sukhdev Singh Dhindse, refused to join the Ministry on account of opposition from Barnala. But he was sworn in next month.

    Sushma Swaraj, formerly a Union Minister and Delhi Chief Minister lost in the election against Sonia Gandhi in Bellary. A protégé of L.K. Advani, she had been promised a membership of Rajya Sabha and a place in the Ministry if she could not make out in the fight against Sonia Gandhi. He was not included in the first stage of Cabinet formation.

99. Shiv Sena leader Bal Thackeray expressed the view that their portfolios were not adequate, The Hindu, Kochi, 15th October 1999.

100. V. Venkatesan: *'A Balacing Act'*, Frontline, 19th November 1999, p.24.

101. *Ibid: 'A Cautious Approach'*, Frontline,19th November 1999, p. 26.

102. *Ibid.,* p. 27.

103. Diesel price was raised by about 40 per cent in October 1999 on the eve of the counting of votes to the Lok Sabha. This precipitated a countrywide strike by Lorry Owners' Association, but the

government stood firm. TDP and JD (U) warned against any rise in prices of kerosene and LPG.

104. For a discussion of the developments relating to the Ayodhya issue see Frontline, 7th January 2000, pp. 4-11.

105. Saba Naqvi Bhaumik: *'The Epic of Doublespeak'*. Outlook, 15th January, 2001, pp. 30-32.

106. *Times of India*, 20th November 2000.

107. Saba Naqvi Bhaumik and Ashis K. Biswas: *'The Bone Collector'*, Outlook, 22nd January 2001, pp. 22-24.

108. *The Hindu,* Kochi, 6th February 2001.

109. *The Hindu,* Thiruvanathapuram, 9th October 1999.

110. *Indian Express,* New Delhi, 22nd April 1998.

111. *Indian Express,* Kochi, 10th May 1998.

112. *The Hindu,* Thiruvanathapuram, 7th March 1999.

113. M.P. Chronicle, Bhopal, 11th May 1998.

114. Times of India, New Delhi, 9th July 1998.

115. Neena Vyas: *'Physician, Heal Thyself'*, The Hindu, 4th April 1999. p.11.

6

The Role of Regional Political Parties of Tamil Nadu in Indian Coalition Politics

Tamil Nadu can lay claim to at least one unique feature in Indian politics – it is the only state in which no national party has ever been in power in the last four decades, to be precise, since 1967. Nothing can illustrate the lasting impact of the 'Dravidian' movement in the state better than this simple fact. Yet, ironically, each of the several pillars on which that movement was built has been dismantled by parties that are offshoots of the movement. The pillars of the movement were anti-Brahminism, an antipathy to the north of India and its predominant language, Hindi, Atheism, Rationalism – none of these is in great evidence today in the inheritors of the Dravidian movement, so much so that Jayalalitha of the AIADMK is herself a Brahmin. Also, her government was one jump ahead of even the BJP in pushing through a law ostensibly aimed at checking forcible religious conversions[1]. As for the hostility to the north, both the DMK and the AIADMK have, since 1998, had alliances with the BJP, a party that was till a few years back almost entirely confined to north India and was seen as the most ardent champion of a unitary nation in which the hegemony of Hindus and Hindi was emphasised.

Tamil Nadu till recently had more political parties represented in the Lok Sabha than almost any other Indian state.

The 39 MPs that the state sent to the Lok Sabha in the 2004 general elections belonged to six political parties. (Uttar Pradesh has representatives of eight parties in the 14th Lok Sabha). In the 1999 elections, however, there were eight parties representing these 39 Lok Sabha constituencies in Tamil Nadu and in the 1998 elections there were nine. Despite this proliferation of parties, the state had not had a coalition government since its inception. Even when alliances have won assembly elections, it had invariably been the case that the leading party in the winning alliance secured a majority of the assembly seats on its own, enabling it to form a government without having to accommodate the junior partners. This pattern changed after the May 2006 elections, in which the DMK – which led the UPA to power in the state – did not have a majority of seats in the assembly, the DMK was well short of a majority. Yet, none of the other coalition partners joined the government which was formed by the DMK.

Till as late as 1998, the only national parties with any presence in Tamil Nadu were the Congress, the CPI and the CPI(M). The BJP had not won even a state assembly seat, leave alone a Lok Sabha constituency in the state. Even the three national parties that did have a presence in the state were in no position to contest on their own and had to align themselves to one of the two main Dravidian parties – the DMK or the AIADMK – to be able to make any significant headway in terms of winning seats in either the assembly or the Lok Sabha. In 1998, Jayalalitha surprised everybody by tying up with the BJP for the Lok Sabha elections. Political pundits, opinion polls and exit polls all suggested that the experiment would be a failure. The results proved all of them completely wrong, with the AIADMK – led alliance winning 36 of the 39 seats in the state. Besides the AIADMK and the BJP, the coalition includes a clutch of smaller parties – many of which had come into being only in the 1990s – like the Marumalarchi Dravida Munnetra Kazhagam (MDMK), the Pattali Makkal Katchi (PMK), the Tamizhaga Rajiv Congress (TRC) and the Janata Party. The BJP had finally managed to register its presence in Tamil Nadu and as subsequent events indicated, it was there to stay. Even today, the BJP would be hard put to win a single seat on its own strength, but since the 1998 general elections the party has made a significant breakthrough–it is no longer considered an 'untouchable' in Tamil Nadu politics.

The reasons for the dominance of the AIADMK and the DMK in Tamil Nadu politics since 1967 lie in a socio-political movement whose origins can be traced back to the Justice Party formed in 1916 in what was then the Madras Presidency of the British Raj. The Justice Party was formed by P. Thyagarayar as a platform for the area's non-Brahmin social elite.[2] In the first general elections in British India held in 1920, the Justice Party won a landslide victory in the Madras Presidency, bagging 63 of the 98 seats. It remained in power in the provincial government for the next 17 years, advocating 'social justice and equality' for all segments of society. E.V. Ramaswamy Naicker (EVR), who was a member of the Indian National Congress, found himself agreeing with the ideology of the Justice Party. He joined the party and started the Non-Brahmin Self-Respect Movement in 1925. In 1944, by which time Naicker was the leader of the party, he renamed the party the Dravida Kazhagam (the Dravidian Federation) and demanded the establishment of an independent state called Dravidasthan. The Dravidian movement had begun.

To the anti-Brahmin thrust of the Justice Party was now added an ideology that defined itself in racial terms. The Brahmins-and the people of north India – were identified with the Aryans, who were invaders, while the non-Brahmins were portrayed as Dravidians and the true descendents of those who had built the Indus Valley Civilisation. So virulent was the Justice Party's opposition to 'the north' and its leaders, that the party saw August 15, 1947 as a 'black day', a day on which the British rulers while leaving the country had left them at the mercy of the north. The Justice Party had demanded that if India were to be granted independence, the south should be carved out as a separate Dravidasthan.

The antipathy to 'Aryans' also extended to hostility to their religion – Hinduism – which was seen as a religion that had sanctified caste oppression, by the Brahmins in particular. Thus, the Dravida Kazhagam campaigned actively against religion, indeed even against the concept of God. The most prominent religious texts of the Hindus – the Ramayana and the Gita – were denounced as part of an Aryan conspiracy to enslave the Dravidians. The DK also launched a campaign for sua-maryadai kalyanan (Self-respect marriages), which were wedding bereft of any of the Sanskritised rituals and hence, of Hindu priests. This again was an attempt to deny the Brahmin any pride of place in the everyday lives of people.

The next plan of the Dravidian movement was a logical corollary of these moves. Language became the central focus of the movement. Tamil was eulogised as the oldest 'living' language in the world and the most 'evolved' of all languages, while Sanskrit and Hindi were presented as impositions by the aggressors from the north. It was this, in fact, that provided the real cutting edge for the Dravidian movement in electoral politics.[3] The Congress, being an all-India party, could hardly have accepted such a hard line linguistic stance. As the party governing India, it was also committed to the attempt to make Hindi a link language nationally.[7] It could perhaps, have shown greater sensitivity towards the suspicions of the Tamil about the attempts to 'impose' Hindi, but it seems to have failed to understand the depth of feelings on this issue.

The language issue was to become the catalyst that precipitated the decline of the Congress in Tamil Nadu and the ascendance of the Dravidian parties. But before that could happen, E.V. Ramasamy Naiker himself had lost the leadership of the movement. A group of young Dravid Kazhagam leaders, led by C.N. Annadurai and including Muthuvel Karunanidhi (both were to later become Chief Ministers of the state) left the party over personal differences with E.V. Ramasamy Naiker. They formed the Dravida Munnetra Kazhagam (DMK) in 1949 which remains to this day one of the two main Dravidian parties in Tamil Nadu.

The first anti-Hindi agitation was launched by E.V. Ramasamy Naiker in 1952, but it was the agitations of 1965 and 1968 that really assumed a mass character. Both were spearheaded by the DMK. In 1965, the Congress was still in power at the centre and in what was then the state of Madras. Its government in Madras cracked down on the agitation, arresting thousands of agitators. This played no small part in the DMK's victory in the 1967 assembly elections – one in which Congress leader K. Kamaraj had boasted that he would win without having to get up from bed. As soon as it came to power, with 'Anna' as the Chief Minister, the DMK government released all those jailed for the anti-Hindi agitation. The very next years, in 1968, another massive agitation against the centre's attempts to imposte Hindi was launched, this time with a sympathetic government running the state. The DMK warned the Congress government in New Delhi that any attempt to impose Hindi would only strengthen the demand for a separate Dravida Nadu (the land of the Dravidians). A group of students leading the anti-Hindi agitation told Prime Minister Indira Gandhi when she met them that she should choose between Hindi and the unity of the nation.

An interesting paradox of Tamil Nadu politics is the fact that in a state in which language has been the major political issue, at least three important political personalities trace their origins from outside the state. M.G. Ramachandran, or MGR as he was popularly called, whose iconic status remains unchallenged, was a Malayalee of Srilankan origin. Jayalalitha, though a Tamil, comes from a family of Brahmins from Mysore. Finally, Rajnikanth is a Marathi who spent the early part of his adult life as a bus conductor in Bangalore before moving to Madras and Tamil films. Throughout MGR's tenure as Chief Minister, the DMK cadre would try to make an issue of the fact that he was not a Tamil, though the leadership would never publicly raise the issue. Yet, the campaign cut no ice with the electorate.[4] Equally, the AIADMK cadre's attempts to counter this by insinuating that Karunanidhi himself was actually a Telugu and not a Tamil left the voters cold.

Having ridden to power on the strength of a movement that was explicitly anti-Brahmin, anti-Religion and anti-North, the DMK gradually diluted each of these agendas. This process picked up pace after the formation of the AIADMK in 1972, when MGR broke away from the DMK. He preferred to focus on projecting the image of the AIADMK as a party of the downtrodden. The ground work for this had, ironically, already been done by his erstwhile mentor M. Karunanidhi, who had written the scripts for most of the films that MGR had starred in. As a conscious political strategy that has perhaps no parallel anywhere in the world, the DMK had systematically used the medium of cinema to project its leaders and its message. MGR had been the prime vehicle for this strategy. In film after film, he appeared either as someone from the working classes or as a benefactor of the working classes – fishermen, rickshaw pullers, landless labourers and so on. Karunanidhi's acknowledged prowess in writing powerful scripts had ensured that MGR was seen as a 'messiah of the people' even before he floated his own political party.

MGR made the most of this image both as the leader of a political party and as Chief Minister of Tamil Nadu after 1977. He also made a conscious effort to specifically target women as a vote bank, coining the term tai kulam (literally, the family of mothers) while referring to them. Arguably the single-most important measure he undertook as Chief Minister was to introduce the mid-day meal scheme in the state. Under the scheme, every child who attended primary school was entitled to a meal in school at the expense of the state. There were additional incentives for girl children in particular. The idea was to provide an economic incentive for poor families to send their children to school rather than to work for a living. To begin with, most economic commentators were aghast at the scheme, derogatorily describing it as 'populist' and arguing that it would place an unsustainable burden on the state's coffers. More than a decade later, even the World Bank, one of the most virulent critics of the mid-day meal scheme when it was introduced, was forced to admit that it has indeed been a major success and more and more status sought to emulate the scheme.

There were others schemes as well that buttressed MGR's image as a messiah of the masses. One scheme was to motorize rickshaws in Chennai which did away with almost all the physical labour involved in plying such vehicles. The other scheme was to construct pucca houses for fisher folk. These schemes became so popular that MGR came to be known as Puratchi Thalaivar (revolutionary leader) and the AIADMK was to stay in power from 1977 to 1989. Many outside Tamil Nadu have simplistically perceived MGR's popularity to be primarily a consequence of his popularity as a film personality. The reality was clearly more complex.

MGR's tenure also saw an interesting innovation being brought into the manner in which electoral alliances were struck. After the creation of the AIADMK, the politics of Tamil Nadu had followed a pattern – the Congress, which by this time had acknowledged that it could not come to power on its own in Tamil Nadu, realised that it could play a decisive role by aligning with either the DMK or the AIADMK. The two Dravidian parties also recognised that the Congress could tilt the electoral balance even if it couldn't do very much on its own. MGR, however, carried this logic a step further. In 1984, when general elections and state assembly elections were held simultaneously, the AIADMK agreed to let the Congress contest as many as 26 of the 39 Lok Sabha constituencies in Tamil Nadu.[5] In the assembly elections, however, the Congress contested only 72 of the 234 seats, while AIADMK candidates contested from as many as 155 constituencies.

This was a radically different approach from what had been practiced all over India till then. Traditionally, the share of seats contested has not been bettered before or since by any alliance in Tamil Nadu. The DMk was left with just two MLAs in the new assembly, one of them the deposed Chief Minister M. Karunanidhi.

The period since then has seen fairly dramatic developments in Tamil Nadu politics. Jayalalitha's first term as Chief Minister saw her adopt an imperious style of functioning that has now become her trademark. Stories abound of how even senior ministers and party leaders would not be allowed to sit at the same level as 'amma' on a dais during public meetings. They would also publicly touch her feet and make it a point to sing praises of the puratchi thalaivi at every opportunity. The state's bureaucracy too learned how not to offend the Chief Minister in any way, since she could be extremely humiliating. Jayalalithaa was also perceived as a corrupt leader, one who used power to confer undue favours on those close to her, including, above all, Sasikala Natarajan, a woman who had almost overnight become her close confidante and was seen as an extra-constitutional authority in the state. A southern industrialist, Rajarathinam, who emerged as a take-over tycoon out of the blue, was also seen as a front man for Jayalalitha.

The incident that did most damage to Jayalalithaa's reputation, however, was the marriage of Sasikala's son in 1995. The streets of Chennai through which the wedding procession was to pass were decorated in a manner reminiscent of royal weddings of yore. Plantain trees in hundreds were cut down in various parts of the state and planted along the route of the procession and the state machinery was blatantly used for the organisation of the lavish ceremony. Many residents of Chennai who witnessed the extravaganza first-hand were shocked at the pomp and show, but the DMK made sure this sense of shock was not confined to Chennai alone. Sun TV, the most popular private television channel in the state and one that is owned by former DMK leader Murasoli Maran's family, spared no effort in ensuring that the pictures of this outrageous splurge reached every corner of the state. If films were the medium for the political message in Tamil Nadu till the 1980s, TV subsequently emerged to grab that role. If the DMK could depend on Sun for propaganda, Jaya TV made sure Jayalalithaa's views reach the masses.

As the 1996 Lok Sabha and state assembly elections drew near, it had become increasingly clear that Jayalalithaa's charisma had begun to fade and that voters were disillusioned with her government and fed up with her autocratic and corrupt ways. The Congress leadership in the state, having seen the writing on the wall, tried to persuade the central leadership of the party that striking an alliance with the AIADMK for the elections would prove suicidal. P.V. Narasimha Rao, who was then Prime Minister and Congress president, however, insisted on an electoral pact with Jayalalithaa. This led to a revolt in the state unit, with almost the entire local leadership quitting the Congress to form the Tamil Maanila Congress (TMC). The TMC then struck an alliance with the DMK. In the assembly elections that followed, the DMK-TMC alliance romped to victory, winning 212 of the 234 seats. Tamil Nadu had rejected Jayalalithaa almost as decisively as it had voted her to power just five years earlier.

Among the first things the DMK government (the TMC did not join the government, but supported it from outside) did after assuming power was to get the state administration to institute a slew of corruption cases against Jayalalithaa, charging her with impropriety in land allotments, import of coal, foreign exchange transactions and so on. Special courts were set up to deal with these cases on the grounds that they involved the larger public interest and could not be allowed to proceed at the languid pace at which cases normally proceed in India's logjammed judicial system.[6] At the behest of the DMK government, police officials raided her residence at Poes Garden. The media was treated to detailed accounts of the number of sarees she possessed, not to mention pairs of shoes and jewellery. These were also shown on the Sun channel and she was sought to be derogatorily portrayed as an Indian version of Imelda Marcos, the late Filipino dictator's wife with a reputation for a fondness for the good things in life.

Jayalalithaa was arrested and put in jail. This, as later events proved, was an error of judgement on the part of the DMK government. As with Indira Gandhi in the immediate aftermath of the Emergency, public anger against Jayalalithaa soon turned to sympathy for a woman who was seen as being hounded by her political opponents. Jayalalithaa contributed to this by portraying herself as a defense less woman who was being made to suffer in jail like an ordinary criminal as part of a politically motivated witch-hunt. However, she also realised that mere public sympathy would not be enough to undo the damage that the cases against her could do. For that, she would need acess to the levers of power.

In 1998, she took the plunge by striking an alliance with the BJP and a host of smaller parties that had sprung up in the state during the mid-1990s. Most analysts and political pundits were dismissive of this alliance. The BJP, it was pointed out, was rather weak in time in 1996. The other partners in the AIADMK –led alliance included fledgling regional parties like the Pattali Makkal Katchi (PMK), the Marumalarchi DMK and the Tamizhaga Rajiv Congress, none of which were expected to make a major contribution to the cause of the alliance. Opinion polls and exit polls conducted before and during the 1998 Lok Sabha elections seemed to bear out the prognostication of political analysts that the AIADMK-led alliance would not perform well. The results, however, proved the pollsters and the pundits completely wrong-Jayalalithaa's electoral strategy proved to be a winner with the AIADMK-led alliance winning 30 of the 39 Lok Sabha seats in the state.

In retrospect, a series of bomb blasts in Coimbatore on February 14, 1998, the day L.K. Advani was to address an election meeting in that city, appear to have played a significant role in catalysing the switch in voter preference towards the AIADMK and the BJP. The blasts, which were the handiwork of an organisation of Muslim fundamentalists, served the AIADMK-BJP alliance at two different level.[7] At one level, they helped the BJP polarise voters along communal lines not only in Coimbatore, but also in other parts of the state where it had till that stage a marginal presence. At another level, it helped the alliance portray the DMK government as being inept and reluctant to deal with the menace of terrorism.

The AIADMK with 18 MPs turned out to be the single largest ally of the BJP in the second Vajpayee government that came to power in New Delhi in March 1998. Jayalalithaa used her clout from the word go-she delayed providing a formal letter of support to the Vajpayee government till almost the final hour. Then, she demanded that her nominees (including Dr Subramaniam Swamy of the Janata Party who had, ironically, earlier been responsible for instituting a number of criminal cases against her) be allocated key portfolios in the Union government. As a matter of fact, she even demanded that Dr Swamy be made Finance Minister, a demand that was rejected by Vajpayee and his supporters (including Jaswant Singh who had gone to Chennai to negotiate with Jayalalithaa). The AIADMK general secretary did, however, succeed in having her party's MPs Union Law Minister and Minister of State for Finance.

What became evident in no time at all was that these Ministers had a single-point agenda: to ensure that the criminal cases against their leader were either dropped or placed in cold storage. Minister of State for Finance, R.K. Kumar, who was in charge of Revenue, Banking and Insurance, did his bit for his leader by transferring a number of income tax officers. However, Jayalalithaa asked him to resign in May 1998. The ostensible reason was that his health was rather poor. It was another matter that speculation was rife that the real reason for his removal was that Jayalalithaa felt he hadn't done what she had expected of him. Another AIADMK leader, K.M.R. Janarthanan, who was earlier Minister of State for Personnel and Grievances in the Vajpayee government, later got Kumar's job in the Finance Ministry. Another AIADMK Minister, Sedapatti Muttaiah, who held the Surface Transport portfolio, had to quit within weeks of his becoming Minister for different reasons – a court hearing the corruption cases against AIADMK leaders passed strictures against Muttaih for allegedly acquiring assets disproportionate to his known sources of income.

Law Minister M. Thambidurai transferred large numbers of legal officers in Tamil Nadu. Jayalalithaa's supporters wanted to transfer some of the criminal cases pending against her from the special courts in Chennai to the Supreme Court in New Delhi, the game plan was to try and ensure that the state government would not remain the prosecuting authority. Jayalalithaa's lawyers also sought to convince the apex court of the country that the criminal cases against her had been politically motivated and should, therefore, be dropped and the special courts be disbanded.

The Supreme Court did not accept the AIADMK's plea that the case against Jayalalithaa should be moved from Chennai to New Delhi. She and her supporters then stepped up their demands for a dismissal of the Karunanidhi-led DMK government in Tamil Nadu under Article 356 of the Constitution of India. The Coimbatore blasts and the DMK's alleged softness towards the perpetrators of that crime were presented as the reason for invoking Article 356. Vajpayee and other senior leaders of the Union government refused to play ball. Having always protested against the misuse of Article 356 by Union governments led by the Congress, they argued, they could not now turn around and apply the same constitutional provision on the flimsiest of excuses to dismiss a democratically elected state government. The friction between the BJP and the AIADMK that was to ultimately result in the fall of Vajpayee's government in April 1999 had reached a critical point.

The dispute between Tamil Nadu and Karnataka over the sharing of the waters of the River Cauvery (also spelt Kaveri) became another issue on which the Vajpayee government found itself facing pressure from Jayalalithaa. For the BJP had made significant inroads in recent years. The party also believed at that time that it could split the ruling Janata Dal in Karnataka and further enhance its presence in the state. The Vajpayee government could not, therefore, adopt a stand on the sensitive issue of apportioning the waters of the Cauvery (especially during the summer months) that would be seen to be against Karnatak's interests. On the other hand, taking a position that was entirely supportive of Karnataka would nip in the bud any prospects the BJP had of making headway in Tamil Nadu, a state in which the party had only just managed to register its presence. Jayalalithaa also spotted in the controversy an opportunity to embarrass an ally who had refused to give in to all her demands, while simultaneously scoring political points against her main political opponent in the state, the DMK and its Chief Minister M. Karunanidhi. She, therefore, adopted a hard line stance, accusing the centre of being deliberately partisan towards Karnataka and the DMK state government of not doing enough to protect the interests of the farmers of Tamil Nadu's Cauvery delta.

Jayalalithaa also took exception to the dismissal of Chief of the Navy, Admiral Vishnu Bhagwat.[8] This was a clear sign that the AIADMK leader was increasingly distancing herself from the Vajpayee government, since the then Defence Minister Fernandez had often acted as an emissary between the Prime Minister and her, and was seen as having a better rapport with her than many others in the Vajpayee government.

It was a matter of time before the rapidly deteriorating relationship between the AIADMK and the BJP finally fell apart. Matters came to a head in April 1999, ultimately leading to the fall of the government. However, Jayalalithaa's gameplan did not succeed fully. The AIADMK supreme did not have the friendly government in New Delhi that she had so desperately tried to bring about. The criminal cases instituted against her continued to do the rounds of courtrooms.

In the September-October 1999 Lok Sabha elections, political alliances in Tamil Nadu had changed drastically from what they were a year earlier. The BJP was now in an alliance with the

DMK, as were smaller parties like the PMK, the MDMK and the TRC. The TMC, earlier the DMK's partner, refused to have anything to do with an alliance that included the BJP. On the other hand, the Congress and the left parties being in alliance with the AIADMK meant that the TMC could not be part of that front either. After all, the very existence of the TMC was due to the fact that its leaders had left the Congress because of its tie-up with the AIADMK. Thus, the TMC was left out in the cold, having to contest more or less on its own, though it had an alliance with the Puthizha Tamizhagam (PT), a party that was trying to build itself as a representative of the dalits, much like the BSP in Uttar Pradesh.

The results of the 1999 elections in Tamil Nadu were not quite as decisive as had been the trend in the state. The DMK-led NDA won 26 of the 39 seats, but the AIADMK-led alliance also managed to win 13 seats. The TMC, not surprisingly, drew a blank. In 2001, Jayalalithaa became the first Chief Minister to be convicted and sentenced in a criminal case of corruption.[9] The case involved allotment of land by a state government undertaking, the Tamil Nadu Small Industries Corporation (TANSI), allegedly at throwaway prices, to a company associated with the Chief Minister. Jayalalithaa's lawyers appealed against the special court's decision in the High Court but before the court decided on the appeal, assembly elections were notified to take place in May 2001. It was generally believed that the AIADMK would be able to defeat the DMK in the elections. Jayalalithaa becoming the next Chief Minister of Tamil Nadu seemed an almost foregone conclusion. She filed her nomination as a contestant from four separate constituencies-Krishnagiri, Pudukottai, Andipatti and Bhuvanagiri-but her nomination papers were rejected in all four constituencies.

In Krishnagiri and Andipatti, her nomination papers were rejected on the ground that she had been convicted in a criminal case and hence could not contest elections under Section 8(3) of the Representation of People Act, 1951. Jayalalithaa's lawyers argued that since she had filed an appeal against her conviction in the higher court, she should be allowed to contest the elections. The returning officer of the constituency from where she had filed her nomination, on the other hand, ruled that as a convicted individual she was not eligible to contest the elections under the provision of the Act. The fact that she had filed an appeal against the conviction, the returning officers pointed out, did not imply that the conviction was no longer valid. In Bhuvanagiri and Pudukotti, the returning officers rejected her nomination on the ground that Section 37(7) (b) of the Act prohibited a person from contesting elections from more than two constituencies simultaneously.

The dispute on Section 8(3) went to the Supreme Court, which stated that during an election, the ruling of the returning officer was final. Any appeal against the officer's order could be made only after the elections had been concluded. Jayalalithaa was thus unable to contest the assembly elections that saw the AIADMK emerging as the ruling party-the party on its own won 132 seats and with its allies (the Congress, the left parties and the PMK) won 173 seats in the 234 member assembly. Jayalalithaa was sworn in as Chief Minister because the law provided for a person who was not an elected member of the assembly to become a Chief Minister provided such a person was elected to the assembly within a period of six months. The decision of Tamil Nadu Governor Fatima Beevi to swear Jayalalithaa in as Chief Minister despite her conviction drew a lot of flak not just from the DMK and the BJP, but also from several legal luminaries and political leaders. The critics pointed out that as the first woman to become a judge of the Supreme Court, Beevi should have known better than to interpret the law in the manner in which she did. So much so, that the Governor was eventually asked by the Union government to put in her papers. However, Jayalalithaa continued as Chief Minister even after Beevi was replaced.

Jayalalithaa nevertheless needed to get elected to the state assembly by November 2001, when the six-month deadline would run out. Unfortunately for her, the High Court did not decide on her appeal against her conviction in the TANSI land case by that time. Jayalalithaa appealed to the Supreme Court to ask the High Court to expedite its decision, but the highest court of the land refused to intervene. Hence, she had no choice but to step down as Chief Minister. The question upper-most in the minds of most political analysts was whom would she nominate to act as stand-in Chief Minister. In her characteristically imperious style, Jayalalithaa deliberately chose O. Panneerselvam, a first-time MLA to succeed her. Not only was Panneerselvam too junior to harbour any ambitions of his own, he was also a 'dependable' stand-in because he was a protégé of T.T.V. Dinakaran, the nephew of Jayalalithaa's confidante Sasikala and a member of the Lok Sabha.

Soon thereafter, the Chennai High Court upheld Jayalalithaa's appeal against her conviction in the TANSI land case, thereby clearing the way for her to become Chief Minister once again. She was subsequently elected to the assembly from Andipatti.[10] Soon after she returned as Chief Minister in March 2002, Jayalalithaa left nobody in doubt that the DMK and others in the Opposition would have to pay for the 'wrongs' done to her during the DMK's stint in power. A slew of corruption cases were filed against Karunanidhi and some of those who had been ministers in his government. Officials who were seen as close to the DMK were transferred en masse. The extent to which Jayalalithaa's quest for revenue' would go became clear when policemen arrested Karunanidhi from his home in the middle of the night. The DMK alleged that the septuagenarian leader had been manhandled by policemen and Sun TV repeatedly broadcast shots of Karunanidhi being bodily lifted to the waiting police vehicle while crying out for help. Karunanidhi would not spend too much time in jail, but the drama had made its point – Jayalalithaa would not pull punches in her battle against the DMK and its top leadership.

Any doubts on this score were settled when the AIADMK used its majority in the assembly to push through legislation which prohibited the same person from being a member of the legislative assembly and holding the post of mayor at the same time. It was no secret that the law was aimed specifically at M.K. Stalin, Karunanidhi's son and heir apparent. Stalin was at that time Mayor of Chennai as well as an MLA. Despite the passage of the law, Stalin refused to resign from either post. He was then disqualified from holding the post of Mayor.

Subsequently, in July 2002, the Tamil Nadu government threw another bombshell when it had V. Gopalaswamy (who prefers to be known as Vaiko) arrested under POTA on the ground that he had made speeches supportive of the banned LTTE. The MDMK leader had been among the most vociferous in supporting the enactment of POTA, in particular arguing strongly in Parliament that it had enough safeguards to prevent its misuse for partisan political purposes. (Ironically, having spent 19 months in jail and having been part of the UPA's clean sweep of the seats in Tamil Nadu in the 2004 Lok Sabha elections, Vaiko had no compunctions in joining the AIADMK in an alliance for the assembly elections of May 2006. He and his party, however, continued to remain part of the UPA in New Delhi).

At the time of Karunanidhi's arrest, together with two of his party colleagues who were central ministers, the Union Law Minister Arun Jaitley had argued that a grave constitutional impropriety had been committed. A state government, he insisted, could not arrest central ministers without the permission of the Union government. The governor of Tamil Nadu was asked for a report on the law and order situation in the state, the underlying threat being that the central government could invoke the provisions of Article 356 to dismiss the state government. When Vaiko was arrested, on the other hand, the BJP restricted itself to making statements to the effect that the use of POTA may have been inappropriate in this case. The reason for the strangely subdued tone of the protest was not very hard to find. Jayalalithaa had by the time of Vaiko's arrest started making overtures to the BJP, clearly indicating that she was willing to forget the acrimony of the part and build new bridges with the Vajpayee government.

The message became increasingly louder thereafter. One of the clearest signals was when Jayalalithaa, during a press conference in Delhi, 'volunteered' the information that she was against Sonia Gandhi becoming Prime Minister because she was born an Italian. Considering that the press conference was taking place after a meeting convened by the Prime Minister to discuss the Cauvery waters dispute between Tamil Nadu and Karnataka, Jayalalithaa's unsolicited comment on the Congress president's Italian origins acquired considerable political significance. In December 2002, Jayalalithaa was the only Chief Minister whose party was not a member of the NDA to be invited to the swearing in ceremony of Gujarat Chief Minister Narendra Modi and the only one to attend it. The AIADMK supreme also gladdened the BJP by enacting a law in Tamil Nadu ostensibly aimed at preventing 'forcible' religious conversions. Modi approvingly cited Tamil Nadu's example and promised to follow suit by enacting a similar law in Gujarat.

While these moves by Jayalalithaa were signs of a growing closeness between the AIADMK and the Vajpayee government, they were also a telling indicator of how drastically 'Dravidian' politics has changed over time. The AIADMK today is indistinguishable in its ideology (and to a large extent so is the DMK) from any of the other mainstream parties in India. The anti-Brahminical thrust, the shunning of ritual and religion, the demonisation of the north of India, are all at best fast fading memories.

This perhaps also explains the fragmentation of Tamil Nadu's polity in recent years. The reasons for the formation of each of the many new parties in the state may vary, but ideology certainly doesn't appear to be the motive force. The MDMK, for instance, was formed because Vaiko, who was one of the most prominent young leaders in the DMK, could see that the rise of Stalin under Karunanidhi's patronage made his progress within the party hierarchy extremely unlikely.[11] The PMK arose as a party restricted to espousing the cause of the Vaniyars, an intermediate caste group accounting for a significant part of the population in some of the northern districts of Tamil Nadu. The Puthiya Tamizhagam (PT) has emerged as a party specifically focusing on dalits, though it is yet to make much headway. In the heyday of the Dravidian movement, these were all groups who saw their aspirations find expression within the Dravidian fold.

At the same time as these small groups have been breaking away, the DMK and the AIADMK have been trying to extend their influence beyond their traditional vote banks to groups like the Brahmins. Interestingly, the beginning of a similar phenomenon is discernible in the caste-polarised polity of states like Uttar Pradesh and Bihar, where the SP, BSP and RJD are all attempting to woo voters from the upper castes as well.

In the May 2004 Lok Sahba elections, the DMK-led alliance had thrashed the AIADMK coalition by wining all the 40 Lok Sabha seats in the state as well as in Pondicherry. Unlike the left, which chose to support the UPA government in New Delhi from outside, the DMK became a significant partner of the Congress in the UPA. This shock woke Jayalalithaa up. In the months that followed, the former Tamil Nadu Chief Minister unleashed a series of programmes aimed at wooing the poor and very poor. She offered free books to any student, girl or boy, up to Class XII. She also offered Rs. 500 to every woman who reported pregnant at the local government hospital. If the woman delivered a child, she got an additional Rs. 5,000. This was aimed at trying to end the practice of female foeticide in Tamil Nadu. With a slew of other schemes, Jayalalithaa ensured that every poor family got at least one monetary offering a month.

In the first week of March, she managed to break the DMK-led alliance when she got Vaiko to her side. This was the same Vaiko whom Jayalalithaa had kept in prison under the Terrorist and Disruptive Activitites Act (TADA) for 19 months because Vaiko was said to have spoken to Tamil activists from Sri Lanka who belong to the LTTE. The State government had also been complimented for its efforts during the relief and rehabilitation of the victims of the tsunami of December 2005.

Despite the AIADMK's attempts to match the DMK in announcing populist schemes, such as providing rice at Rs 2 per kg and free television sets, Jayalalithaa and her party lost the assembly polls in May 2006. She had tried very hard to change her image of being a haughty and arrogant leader. After dismissing many striking State government employees, she agreed to reinstate them. None of these moves eventually helped her in the assembly elections. The DMK emerged as the single largest party in Tamil Nadu after polling 26.45 per cent of the votes and winning 96 seats. Its biggest ally, the Congress, won 34 seats, a huge improvement from 2001 when the party won only seven seats. The alliance obtained 44.73 per cent of the votes, around 4.7 per cent more than its opposing coalition.

Tamil Nadu politics has been influenced greatly by its film personalities, as already mentioned. In 2006, a new political outfit headed by a film personality, Vijayakant, the Desiya Murpokku Dravida Kazhagam (DMDK), played the role of spoiler by fielding candidates in as many as 206 out of the 234 seats in the assembly; the party's candidates were placed third in many constituencies and indirectly worked towards the defeat of AIADMK candidates.[12] In fact, the DMDK polled 8.38 per cent of the total votes polled in the state, which was almost equal to the vote share of the Congress and four times more than the vote share of the BJP (2.02 per cent).

Another newly floated party that entered the electoral fray for the first time was the Lok Paritrana party that was led by former and current students of the Indian Institute of Technology at Chennai. This party sought to make a point that educated individuals should enter politics. However, the best a candidate of the party could do was to be placed in third position in the post Anna Nagar constituency in Chennai.

An interesting fallout of the 206 assembly elections in Tamil Nadu has been that the Congress and the DMK have become more dependent on each other. The DMK is for the first time heading a minority government in the state with the Congress as one of its partners, while the DMK is an important constituent of the UPA government in New Delhi.

Dramatic events May 2007 illustrated both the problems that are likely to confront the DMK after Karunanidhi is no longer around as well as the maner in which coalition partners 'nominate' their members to hold ministerial positions in New Delhi, irrespective of what the Prime Minister might want.[13] In early May, Dayanidhi Maran, who was then Union Minister for Communications & Information Technology, had to resign following a factional fight within his own party, the DMK, that claimed three lives.

The problem started with the Tamil daily, Dinakaran, publishing an opinion poll on who should succeed Karunanidhi when he hands over the reins of the party. According to the poll, the younger of the DMK chief's two sons from his second wife, M.K. Stalin, was chosen by 70 per cent of the respondents, while Stalin's elder brother M.K. Azhagiri and Karunanidhi's youngest daughter, Kanimozhi (from his third wife) got barely two per cent support each from those polled. An undefined group of 'others' was supported by 20 per cent. Azhagiri's supporters saw this as an attempt by the Marans, who own the Dinakaran and the Sun media group (the largest conglomerate of its kind in southern India, headed by Dayanidhi's elder brother Kalanidhi), to marginalise him and to indirect promote Dayanidhi's own claims to succeeding Karunanidhi. They went on a rampage attacking the Dinakaran office on the outskirts of Madurai with petrol bombs. Two systems engineers and a security guard died in the resulting fire.

The fracas detracted from what was supposed to have been a period of grand celebration for Karunanidhi – he had just completed 50 years in the state assembly and his 84th birthday was to follow soon on June 3.

Far from condemning the Azhagiri faction's strong-arm tactics, the DMK leadership threw its weight behind the Chief Minister's family and demanded that action be taken against Dayanidhi – himself a grandnephew of Karunanidhi. Dayanidhi had no option but to resign as Union Minister even as he kept insisting that he would remain a supporter of the DMK till the day he died. He told journalists how he as a Union Minister had been responsible for bringing to Tamil Nadu major investments made by multinational telecommunications firms. While Dayanidhi denied that he had promoted his brother's business interests, it is also correct that the Sun group had drawn up ambitious expansion plans not only in the media (including a tie-up with a Rupert Murdoch-controlled organisation) but also in aviation. Dayanidhi hinted that his hope of making a major announcement-abolishing of 'roaming' charges within India for users of mobile telephones-on Karunanidhi's birthday had been dashed. The Chief Minister's loyalists in the DMK accused Dayanidhi of over-stepping his limits by calling up the Home Secretary in the State government 'threatening' him with stern action if he did not apprehend the 'real' culprits behind the arson and violence in the Madurai office of Dinakaran.

The Prime Minister had no option but to acquiesce in the exit of Dayanidhi from the Union Cabinet and wait for the DMK to nominate someone to replace him. Interestingly, the DMK actually settled for the Cabinet post less than it earlier had. While A. Raja, who was Union Minister for Forests and Environment was given Dayanidhi's portfolio, the new DMK person inducted, M.K. Selvi, was given only a Minister of State rank.[14] Both ranks and portfolios were decided by the DMK, not Manmohan Singh.

What this episode made evident was that in coalition governments, there is an unwritten rule that partners have specific quotas 'reserved' for them in the Union Cabinet and Council of Ministers and it is up to them and not the prerogative of the Prime Minister to decide who should hold which of these posts.

References

1. Eugene Irschick: *'Politics and Social Conflict in South India: The Non-Brahmin Movement and Tamil Separatism – 1916-1929'*, University of California Press, Berkeley, 1969.

2. The Self-Respect League, founded by E.V. Ramaswami Naicker, was the organisation most actively involved in radical propaganda.

3. V. Subramaniam: *'Emergence and Eclipse of Tamil Brahmins : Some Guidelines to Research'*, Economic and Political Weekly, July 1969, Vol. 4, Nos. 28-30, pp.1133-1136.

4. Stephen A. Barnett: *'Urban is an Urban Does: Two Incidents on One Street in Madras, South India'*, Urban Anthropology, Fall 1973, Vol. 2, No. 2, pp. 129-160.

5. Several sources exist on the political mobilisation of lower castes in Tamil Nadu. For a study of the Vanniya Kula Kshatriyas see Lloyd I. Rudolph and Susanne Hoeber Rudolph. *'The Modernity of Tradition'*, University of Chicago Press, Chicago 1967 and for an account of Nadar political history which includes discussion of their party involvement see Robert L. Hardgrave, Jr., *The Nadars of Tamil Nadu: Political Culture of a Community in Change*, University of California Press, Berkeley, 1969. Marguerite Ross Barnett, The Politics of Cultural Nationalism discusses comparative caste mobilisation in the context of British policy and the Dravidian and Congress movement ideologies.

6. C. N. Annadurai had been a popular leader of the Dravida Kazhagam and editor of the important journal, Dravida Nadu (Dravidian country). He later became an extremely popular leader and Chief Minister of Tamil Nadu in 1967. He died in February, 1969.

7. In general, the early Dravidian movement organisations had more support in the Tamil-Speaking areas of Madras Presidency than in the Telugu-Speaking areas.

8. Both were Tamil journals published by Dravidian movement organisations. Kudi Arasu (People's Government) was a Self-Respect League and D.K. Publication. Dravida Nadu (Dravidian Country) was edited by C. N. Annadurai and was both a D.K. and DMK publication.

9. Hardgrave, Robert L.: '*The Dravidian Movement*', Popular Prakashan, Bombay, 1965.

10. Lloyd I. Rudolph: '*Urban Populist Radicalism: Dravidian Politics in Madras*', Journal of Asian Studies, May 1961, Vol. 20, pp. 283-297.

11. Tamil Nadu constituencies were the same in 1967 and 1971. However, between 1957 and 1962 and between 1962 and 1967 constituencies were redrawn. In order to perform longitudinal analyses, constituency matches were made using census and delimitation volumes plus the 1967 and 1971 electoral issues of Madras Information and Tamil Arasu. Both are Tamil Nadu government publications.

12. C.A. Perumal: '*Regionalism and Political Development*', IJPs, Vol. 48, No. 1, 1987, p. 6.

13. Since alliances did not play a strong part in DMK-Congress interaction, Table II: 7 does not include alliance per cent of the vote as a control. The question of DMK and Congress alliances will be taken up below.

14. Narendra Subramanian: '*Ethnicity and Populist Mobilization: Political Parties, Citizens and Democracy in South India*', Oxford University Press, New Delhi, 1999.

7

Summary and Conclusion

The role of the regional political parties in Indian political system has been both functional as well as dysfunctional. On the one hand, they have helped in the development of participatory political culture and provided a check against the dictatorial tendencies of the Union Government and, on the other, they are also a source of strength for the development of federal process. By virtue of being ruling parties in some States and Opposition parties at the Centre their contribution for the successful functioning of Parliamentary democracy is no less important because a political party which rules must also know, how to play the role of an Opposition.

In a parliamentary democracy the minority must have its say, the majority must have its way and the regional parties have played this role successfully by being ruling as well as Opposition parties at the same time. They have also succeeded in exposing the partisan role of the Governors in the appointment and dismissal of the Chief Ministers, in issuing of ordinances, reservation bills for the consideration of the President. Moreover, by fighting against the unchecked entry of foreign nationals, the Assam Gana Parishad has done a really national service. The passing of Lok Ayukta bills in Andhra Pradesh and Karnataka for the prevention of corruption has also put the Congress(I) party in a tight corner and now perhaps it may hasten the process of passing of Lok Pal bill which should bring even the Prime Minister in its purview. Their role is also significant in providing legitimacy to the political process. In the process of political penetration in the far-flung and inaccessible areas particularly in the Tribal belts, the role of regional parties is of special significance.[1]

The role of some of the regional parties has also adversely affected the process of State building and Nation building and unfortunately some of the All-India parties in some cases have also joined hands with such regional parties keeping in view the partisan interests.[2]

Political parties, whether they are national or regional in nature, are one of the important agents of articulating and organising the political forces. In the pre-independence period regionalism was in a dormant stage because of the disorganised nature of the regional forces. In the post-independence period, however, the regional political parties have developed. The federal structure in India while being affected by the nature of the political parties, also affected their nature in turn. This interaction between the party structure and the federal system is evident in the functioning of the party system in the Indian federal polity.

There has been a mushroom growth of the regional parties in India. After the Fourth General Elections of 1967 the Congress lost its monopoly of power both at the Centre and the States. It came to power at the Centre with a reduced majority and the non-Congress governments were formed in many States. The States which were described by some scholars as mere administrative units of the Centre before 1967, came to be assertive. There was a demand for greater autonomy for the states by the non-Congress governments, within the framework of our Constitution.

The regional political parties which undoubtedly represent a centrifugal force in any federal system have been greatly responsible for changing the balance of power in India more particularly after 1967. These parties which were for a long time unarticulated and disorganised, gained strength gradually and manifested themselves for the first time during the 1967 General Elections.

There are others, which are the breakaway factions of the Indian National Congress like the Bangla Congress in West Bengal, Kerala Congress in Kerala and the Jana Congress and the Utkal Congress in Orissa. Most of these regional parties have shared political power in the post-1967 era and have demanded greater autonomy for the states. The most vocal support for the state autonomy came from Akali Dal of Punjab, DMK of Tamil Nadu and the Utkal Congress of Orissa. The leadership was provided in this respect by the DMK government of the erstwhile Madras State and for the first time an well-organised regional party could come to power.[3] Some of the regional parties were also partners in the coalition governments formed in several states after the fourth general elections of 1967.

In the name of greater autonomy of states some regional parties have gone to an extreme extent in their demands. The Shiv Sena in Maharashtra has raised the slogan of the 'Sons of the Soil' and 'Maharashtra for Maharashtrians'. The Akali Dal had been insisting on the fulfilment of the Anandpur Sahib Resolution of 1973. The DMK had been championing the cause of Tamil nationalism and there was a time it was advocating for a separate Dravidian State in the South. This stand was later abandoned in 1962. These slogans posed serious challenges to the federal structure in particular and the unity and integrity of the nation in general.

The demand for State autonomy has been justified on the ground that the State governments are closer to the people and also can serve the people better. This demand was significant in the backdrop of the feeling that the interests of the States have been neglected by the Centre and that it has failed to come up to the expectation of the people.

During the late 1960's series of attempts were made to demand the restructuring of the Center-State relations. The anti-Centre attitude took a new dimension with the slogan of secession by some advocates of greater State autonomy. The growing importance of the States vis-à-vis the centre could seen in the emergence of some political leaders with charisma and mass base. After the 1971 elections the old concept of Congress

Party ruling at the Centre and most of the States was revived. The regional political parties could not effectively raise the slogan of State autonomy. After the 1977 elections to the Lok Sabha, it paved the way for a dialogue for restructuring the Centre-State relations, with the Janata Party at the helm of affairs at the Centre. The Janata Party advocated decentralisation of power but was not prepared to do anything that would weaken the Centre.[4]

In 1977, the Congress lost the political power at the centre and the formation of the first Janata Government at the centre was the result of an accommodative attitude of its constituent political groups. This four party Janata Government headed by Morarji Desai was not technically a coalition because its four constituents had agreed to merge and fight the election on a single manifesto and on a shared symbol. However this Janata Party, which came to power, had declared in its manifesto that there had been "a high degree of centralisation" and it believed in decentralisation of economic and political power. Its first act as the continuation of Congress manipulative politics when it dismissed the Congress governments in the states by invoking Article 356. The states now reasserted their demand for more autonomy. The states of West Bengal, Tamil Nadu, Punjab and Jammu and Kashmir particularly voiced their demands for more powers. A demand was also made to appoint a parliamentary committee to study the center-state relations which was not accepted by the Prime Minister Morarji Desai. The only thing that the Janata government did was scrapping of Article 357A, through 44th constitutional amendment, which had been inserted by the 42nd constitutional amendment, and which enabled the centre to deploy army and para-military force for dealing with any grave situation of law and order in the state.

When the election were held in early 1980 the Congress party once again reemerged with the thumping majority in the parliament thus once again the country comes under the domination of single party-the Indian National Congress(I). Indira Gandhi came back to power and she also got the Janata governments in nine states dismissed through Article 356. Subsequently elections took place in these state assemblies. While Congress came to power in many states but still in a number of states including Andhra Pradesh, Tamil Nadu, Jammu and Kashmir, Karnataka and West Bengal, Non-Congress government were formed where regional parties came into power (the CPM government and the Janata government in Karnataka were also more or less regional party governments). The four Southern states declared the formation of a regional council to buttress the demand for greater state autonomy. In this concern, the Akali Dal was a coalition partner with the Janata Party in the Punjab government between 1977 and 1980, and it did little to raise demands based on the Anandpur Sahib Resolution with the central government. And the beginning of 1980 once again witnessed the reassertion of the Akali's demand for state autonomy. The Akali Dal manifesto at the time of Punjab Vidhan Sabha election in 1980 emphasised the old demand for autonomy for Punjab state and pledged to take away the center's power to dissolve the Vidhan Sabhas.[5] All this led to the appointment of Sarkaria Commission to look into the centre- state relationship in the year 1983.

The controversy over center-state relations in India which had been a lively subject. Particularly since 1967 entered a new phase during Rajiv Gandhi's regime, especially from December 1987 when he began to address District Magistrates and Collectors in different regions, stressing the need to return to a system in which the Collector was to once again become the kingpin of governance. In none of these workshops neither the Chief Ministers of the state, nor anyone from the State governments were involved. This was followed by a plethora of announcements for strengthening Panchayati Raj, speeding up elections to local bodies and constantly emphasising the virtues of 'decentralisation' while at the same time launching virulent attacks on State governments particularly those under opposition rule (but not sparing all Congress (I) run states either).

One of the important positive aspect of Rajiv Gandhi's regime regarding centre-state relations was, the Sarkaria Commission Report (1988) which was appointed by Indira Gandhi by declaring that, the commission would review the centre- state relations within the framework of the constitution was submitted to the government in October 1987 more than four years after the commission's installation under the Prime Ministership of Rajiv Gandhi, kept it under wraps until the end of January 1988.

Participation of many regional parties in the coalition government at the centre from 1989 indicates the reinforcement of significant shift from centralised governance towards shared rule and federal governance.

Barring P.V. Narasimha Rao's minority government which somehow managed the Congress Government, all the other governments that were formed after 1989, have been coalition governments supported by regional parties. V.P. Singh, the Prime Minister of National Front/Janata Dal reactivated the idea of Inter-State Council and set up a secretariat to service it. After him P.V. Narasimha Rao did not pursue it. He even abandoned the practice of calling regular meetings of National Development Council. The Sarkaria Commission, which was submitted in 1988, was also ignored.

A landmark in the development of Indian federalism took place in 1996, when the United Front Government with the support of Congress (I) came to power. This was the government of fourteen regional parties composed of Janata Dal, Communist Party of India (CPI), Communist Party of India (Marxist), Assam Gana Parishad (AGP), Forward Block (FB), Revolutionary Socialist Party (RSP), Samajvadi Party (SP), Telugu Desam Party (TDP), Congress Tiwari, National Conference (NC) and Indian Union Muslim League (IUML). The leader of the United Front H.D. Devegowda himself was a regional leader. Even his colleagues with the exception of P. Chidambaram were regional leaders. The Prime Minister was chosen by the leader of Telugu Desam Party (TDP) and Chief Minister of Andhra Pradesh Nara Chandrababu Naidu. After the fall of Devegowda government, again he along with Harkishan Singh Surjeet (CPM) played the role of kingmaker in installing I.K. Gujral as the Prime Minister.

The novelty of the United Front exercise was that the power shifted from the centre to the state. The state bosses decided who would enter the union ministry from their respective parties and not the Prime Minister. It was also decided by the coalition partners that they would have say in the decision to drop any minister, and also be consulted on the distribution of portfolios. Thus Mulayam Singh Yadav decided the S.P. Ministers in the cabinet. Moopanar the TMC's representative, Chandrababu Naidu those of the TDP, Lalu Yadav of the JD (Bihar), Karunanidhi, the DMK men. Harkishan Singh Surjeet was responsible for B.S. Ramoowalia's entry into the cabinet. It is to be remembered that although Janata Dal, CPM and CPI claim to be National parties but in reality they are regional parties.

The coalition government was functioning on the basis of the document finalised by the constituent regional parties called as the "Common approach to major policy matters and a Minimum Programme" or as it was commonly called the Common Minimum Programme. The most important thing was that for the first time the central government had acknowledged the need to recast centre-state relations.

The Common Minimum Programme "envisaged to advance the principles of political, administrative and economic federalism". It also wanted to go beyond the recommendations of Sarkaria Commission because there has been a new articulation of state rights and the need for greater powers to the states to meet the aspirations of the respective states. "According to the programme, the state should have greater say in determining their priorities in developmental programmes, greater freedom to draw their plans within the broad framework of the national five-year plans. It also stood for the transfer of most of the centrally sponsored schemes to the control of state governments. The document also promised to amend Article 356 to prevent its misuse. It also promised to reactive[6] and energizes institutions like National Development Council and the Inter-State Council. The regional political parties also formed a Federal Front to safeguard the interests of their states.

The United Front experiment failed. The Congress on whose support United Front was in power made its approach to centre-state relationship clear vides its ten-page note on "parameters of support and cooperation" with the United Front.[7] It said, "the scheme of centre-state relationship as adumbrated in our constitution is ideally suited to Indian conditions and is intended to meet the requirements of our pluralist democracy and federal polity. The constitutional system envisages a strong center and strong state and provides full scope for a dynamic relationship between the center and the state. 'Any strong versus weak center' approach is inappropriate and not responsive to the real problems facing the country. There has been in past years an increasing devolution of powers in favour of the states and most of the centrally sponsored schemes are administered by the states. The country's unity and integrity should be of paramount importance".[8]

The BJP-led coalition government marked an advance on the road to coalition politics. A largely pre-election coalition and the one led by a dominant party have a greater chance of survival. Its pre-election alliance were Orissa (BJD), West Bengal (Trinamool Congress), Bihar (Samata party), Haryana (HVP), Punjab (SAD), Maharashtra (Shiva Sena), Andhra Pradesh (TDP-Lakshmiparvati), Karnataka (Lokashakthi) and Tamil Nadu (AIADMK, PMK, MDMK, TRC), then the Haryana Lokdal (Rashtriya) announced to support the former Congress men Buta Singh and Sukhram and another independent member Menaka Gandhi also promised to support. The Arunachal Pradesh Chief Minister offered the support of his two MP's and three others.

Thus the BJP-led coalition in a coalition of too many parties and, infact, factions of parent parties. They all had stronger state agendas and no national agenda. They were little worried how the coalition would fare as long as they gain at the state level. A coordination committee of the coalition was formed but it has been almost defunct.

Burdened with desperate allies and a fractured mandate, Atal Behari Vajpayee struggled to balance conflict with consensus. His major objective was to impart a degree of coherence to a coalition, which was made of parties with individual agenda. The floor text for the Vajpayee government was necessitated on April 14, 1999, the AIADMK, a coalition partner having a strength of 18 members in the Lok Sabha, withdrew its support and a confidence motion moved by Prime Minister Vajpayee lost the confidence motion and resigned.

This BJP-led coalition was very short lived. The novelty of this BJP-led coalition was that the power shifted from the centre to the states. Because all the regional partners of this coalition have their stronger state agendas and there was no national agenda. As a result, states became strong and center became weak.

BJP-led coalition experiment failed very soon 13th Lok Sabha Election was declared in October 1999. This was again a coalition government led by BJP with 24 parties and its biggest coalition partner this time is Telugu Desam Party (TDP). But this time arithmetic is such that even if the TDP withdraws support, the government will not fall. Infact there is little danger to the NDA government unless a group of alliances partners' gang up to brings it down. But potential conspirators will be wary because the opposition is neither strong nor cohesive enough to form a alternative government.

Hence participation of many regional parties in the coalition government at the centre shows the significant shift of federal set up of India. Rajni Kothari in one of the Seminar at New Delhi on March 28, said 'issue of federalism is gaining importance after a long period of ups and downs. For the first time, the BJP seems to be eager to accept the reality of growing regionalisation in politics.[9] It also became evident in the first address of the President to the joint session of parliament on March 25, that Prime Minister A.B. Vajpayee of the BJP and his coalition government would be committed to the 'governance through consensual approach.[10] They would also uphold 'dialogue, debate and discussion' to replace the game of parliamentary majority and minority. Some of the issues in which the new government would like to seek a national consensus urgently are electoral reforms, centre state relations, resolution of inter-state water disputes. The BJP also endorsed the Congress viewpoint, which eliminated the possibility of major changes in the constitution through the constitutional amendment. However, it was almost a sort of revolution when the major governmental policies and decision were to be decided by the regional parties.

In the changed political scenario, the regional parties not only dominated at the centre, they were also in power in many states including Assam, Haryana, Bihar, Orissa, Andhra Pradesh, Tamil Nadu etc. This can also be viewed as the healthy trend towards not only co-operative federalism but also towards national unity. The states may become more responsible and responsive. In Andhra Pradesh, the government attempted to raise its own financial resources by cutting the populist programmes like prohibition. The regional parties are also emphasising the national unity. The Chief Minister of Tamil Nadu declared that the DMK's first goal was to ensure the survival of the country.

However, the new system, at least for the time being, has thrown up a dynamism in which major parties or party-like formations the Congress, the Janata Dal and its National Front allies, the BJP and its allies seem to be almost equally poised for competition. The left and regional parties may play a balancing role. In this multi-polarity it also seems that Indian politics has entered a coalition phase at least for the near future. The 1999 Lok Sabha Elections saw for the first time, a pre-electoral alliance that obtained a clear majority. State parties aggressively pursuing the developmental interests of their respective states joined hands with the BJP after the dissolution of the 12th Lok Sabha in an alliance, which marks the advent of what Balveer Arora calls, 'electoral federalism' For the first time, a major national party pursued a comprehensive strategy of alliances and seat-sharing arrangements accepting to field fewer candidates in the bargain'[11] and there was a continuous decline of seats of national parties in parliament.

In the previous chapters we also discussed causes for emergence of Regional Parties in Tamil Nadu and their role at the state and national politics. It indicates that when the entire country gave a massive vote to the Congress(I) in 1983 and 1984, Assembly and Parliamentary elections the Tamil Nadu voters also elected Regional Parties candidates to act as the national opposition in the parliament. Indira Gandhi's sympathy wave and the Unity and integrity call, the advocacy of one party rule at centre and the states by Rajiv Gandhi failed to move the Tamil Nadu voters they elected the Regional Parties and their opposition alliance with improved majority of seats and votes.

Thus lastly we can mention that, the political scenario in the country has drastically changed. There has been a demand for restructuring of the center-state relationship, the underlying intention being to lift the states from the present position of excessive dependence and subordination and to give them a larger share of power and authority. This demand is a fairy long-standing one but was stepped up in an organised way after the 1967 election when non-Congress parties came to power in several states. It has been revived after the 1977 assembly poll, and after the emergence of regionalism and coalition governments at the central level, and most states like Tamil Nadu, West Bengal and also Jammu and Kashmir have been the most vocal spokesman of this demand, though it is by no means restricted to the trio only. The West Bengal former Chief Minister, Jyoti Basu, has publicly sought[12] more power for the states saying that his government was handicapped in bringing about any fundamental change in the socio-economic structure of the state in the context of its severely limited powers. The Regional Political Parties in Tamil Nadu too have declared their intention to seek changes in the constitution to confer more powers on the states.

It is now being increasingly recognised that the centre can be strong only if the states are also strengthened. We trust that the imbalance in our federal constitution in this regard will be rectified at an early stage through appropriate constitutional amendments and we shall support all efforts in this direction.[13]

The demand for re-carving the centre-state relations has sometimes taken a rather extreme shape, an instance being, a move to delimit the centre's role to only a few subject of national importance. The geo-political considerations alone demand a sufficiently powerful centre in the first quarter of the 21st century; in addition, the tasks of state building, nation building and development postulate an effectively functioning and viable centre. This of course, does not imply that, there is little justification for reform in the field of centre-state relations. At present, the central government has extended its role considerably in the state's sphere of activities, which ought to be curtailed. Instead of endeavouring to become a state government itself, the centre should provide only professional advice and leadership and strengthen the states, which alone would be a sound course of action in the long run.

So far as federalism in India is concerned the conclusion that emerges is that the Indian Federal system changes according to the changes in the party system and nature of the federal structure depends to a certain extent on the nature of the party organisation. Similarly, the system of coalition governments also has a bearing on centre-state relations in India.

Regional parties have thus grown to be a strong force in modern India. In many states, they are the ruling power and where they are not ruling power, they form a significant force in the opposition. The Regional Political Parties of Tamil Nadu have been playing a most important role both at the centre and State in making and unmaking Governments.

The impact of regional parties in India have been both positive and negative over the decades.

The greatest advantage is that as these parties are restricted to a particular region, they are more in touch with ground realities. They are well aware of the local interests, needs and expectations and more sensitive to them with the result that they can react in an effective manner to fulfil them. Manipulations and other unethical practices within such parties are much less when compared to national parties – these can be easily witnessed or sensed and thus there is greater threat of exposure and ridicule. Regional parties, being more homogenous in composition, rule out diverse, conflicting interests that often clash and result in nothing substantial. These parties, after chartering a course of action, are more liable to successfully follow it. These parties may not be restricted to any one state, which means that two or more states also get united in a cause. This provides a favourable prospect for states, amity when it comes to other issues, like industrial development, river waters sharing, etc. Compare and contrast all these advantages with the inherent disadvantage in national parties which include distance from the ground situation so that their response to regional problems is neither sympathetic nor timely, sacrificing of local interests for national interests, manipulation by vested interests to a great extent, and the preoccupation of the leaders with the question of retaining power.

These general advantages of regional parties' aside, in India such parties have played a crucial and positive role in specific ways. This has been mainly in response to the problems created by the one-party dominant rule at the Centre and in the States in post-independent India.

(i) These parties have succeeded in altering the indifferent, apathetic attitude of the common people towards the political process as a result of a long spell of one-party rule. Regional parties, by bringing regional issues especially those of immediate concern to the foreground, have inspired the people to take an active interest in politics.

(ii) In electoral politics, Congress continued in power without any stiff and sustained opposition from other national parties. If such a scenario had continued, it would have proved very unhealthy for our democratic set-up. The regional parties, thankfully, succeeded in providing a genuine challenge to the dominant party. The Akali Dal in Punjab, the National Conference (in Jammu and Kashmir), the DMK and AIADMK (in Tamil Nadu), the Mizo National Front, Assam Gana Parishad (in Assam), the Sikkim Parishad, the Manipur Hill Union and the Manipur Peoples Party (in Manipur) are some examples of regional parties that have been dominant in states. These parties have thus ensured a competitive electoral process.

(iii) The one-party rule has threatened to affect the federal process. The autonomy of the states was in much danger owing to the dominant party's misuse of powers against states ruled by other parties through practices such as arbitrary dismissal of governors and state governments. But the emergence of the regional parties has meant parties that fight for state rights. Steps to review and improve Centre-State relations through the appointment of the Sarkaria Commission and other Acts was a direct result. Strong regional parties have thus saved the federal process from disintegrating.

(iv) Regional parties have time and again, strongly opposed the dominant national party/parties on many issues, forcing the latter to adopt a reasonable approach for conflict resolution. They have exposed a number of failures in our present-day political functioning, such as the misuse of power of issuing ordinances.

Regional parties, by their very definition, are encouragement's to a trend of sub-nationalism that, when exercised without a balance, is bound to affect the unity and integrity of a nation. The 'regional' causes are narrow-based. They aim at the betterment of a specific region only often, as is evident nowadays, opposing the same goal for other regions. The larger cause of the nation is ignored, sometimes intentionally, to win the interests of a region. In the long term, it is the country's oneness that is threatened as regional causes come in conflict and incite passions. Reflect upon the many river waters sharing disputes between two or more states in recent years that have proved an obstacle to development. Many of the parties do not hesitate to encourage violence or pursue violent means and methods themselves to win their goals. Many parties are openly terrorist or secessionist in nature. Such parties have been operating in the northeast, Jammu and Kashmir, Punjab and other states. What is more, they grow by the day! The fact that regional parties, illegitimate in their demands and the means to achieve them in many cases, and often formed by selfish politicians simply to win power, do succeed in winning power has prompted even national parties to embrace so-called 'regional' causes, depending upon the region concerned. This is not a healthy trend as, now even the national parties are therefore proving themselves less committed to pursue national objectives.

It is our historical experience that makes many of us despair of the recent growth and successes of regional parties. We put our faith in national parties, aware that it was only a lack of strong power at the centre and disunity among the various regions that resulted in repeated invasions of the country in the past. The Mughals, the Rajputs, the Marathas and the Sikhs were very powerful regional forces that nevertheless, could not deter the aims of the British in India. It is for this reason that our constitution-makers opted for the creation of a strong central government. The need for this is paramount in a diverse entity like India. The view prevalent in some minds that it is time the regional parties are allowed to take the upper hand in politics cannot be encouraged. According to this view, the country has undertaken economic liberalisation and it is time for a totally decentralised polity now. Centralised politics is not viable and effective any longer. It is also stated that regional parties have been made to realise that violence cannot pay any longer and the country would not tolerate secessionist designs. But this is to be much doubted.

The only possible answer lies in ensuring a strong centre and the success of national parties while encouraging regional parties to an extent that does not hinder the unity, integrity and overall development of the nation. For this, regional parties, which to a large degree excite regional passions, ought to be kept in check. First of all, regional parties that have no genuine and clear agenda for the betterment of a region should not be allowed to proliferate. Many factors have contributed to discourage regionalism and thus large-scale growth of local or regional parties. Increasing political consciousness, the patterns of urbanisation and industrialisation that have been emerging such as the growth of cities, development of transport and communications impact of western culture have resulted in some checks on regionalism. Some measures can be enforced for this purpose. There may include a thorough review of Centre-State relations, reform of our administrative and economic set-up, promoting an educational system that would expose the evils and deteriorate influence of communalism, casteism, linguistic divisions, regional conflicts, etc. Where the regional parties are concerned, as already mentioned, they should be allowed to emerge only on the basis of genuine programmes-that is, those concerned with the socio-economic development of a people. Strict rules and regulations for their formation, working and expanding would prove a significant step. In this context, we must note that political parties in general are subjected to strict and regulated norms for functioning. A reform of our political parties and the people who run them is vital for checking the malaise of regionalism as well as other problems in the Indian political scene.

The regional political parties which are taking initiative in the crucial political issues would contribute largely to determine the future of Indian Federal System and Indian Political Process.

The regional parties are now a force to be reckoned within the Indian Politics. They are now taking initiative in vital issue and more particularly in the centre-state relations. The regional parties particulary of Tamil Nadu are now considered indispensable in providing a viable national alternative even to the Congress Party.

References

1. V. Baskar Rao, B. Venkateshwaralu: '*Parliamentary Democracy in India; Trends and Issues*', Mittal Publication, New Delhi, 1987, p.161.

2. *Ibid.*

3. H.H. Das: '*Federal and State Politics in India*', Discovery Publishing House, New Delhi-1990, pp. 23-24.

4. *Ibid.*, p. 25.

5. Shironami Akali Dal the Chon Patter: '*Manifesto of Akali Dal*', Punjab Vidhan Sabha, 1980, pp. 3-6.

6. Malhotra, Inder: '*Centre State Relations; need for a sense of proportion*', *The Times of India*, March 31st, 1983.

7. Awasthy S.S.: '*Indian Constitution and Politics*', Har-Anand Publications, New Delhi, 1999, p.134.

8. *Ibid.*, p.135.

9. Khan, Arshi: '*Regional Political Parties and New Coalition*', The Radical Humanist, Vol. 62, No. 3, June 1998, p. 4.

10. *Ibid.*

11. Balveer, Arora: '*Political Parties and Party System, the emergence of New Coalition*', Memo, Dec. 1999, pp. 8-9.

12. *The Times of India*, New Delhi, 10th July 1977.

13. *The Hindustan Times*, New Delhi, 8th July 1977.

Bibliography

1. Ambedkar, B.R., (1939). *Federation vs. Freedom* (Bombay : Shree Laxmi Narayan Press).

2. Arora, B. (2000). 'Negotiating differences: federal coalitions and national cohesion', in F. Frankel, Z. Hasan, R. Bhargava and B. Arora (eds) *Transforming India: Social and Political Dynamics of Democracy*, Oxford: Oxford University Press, 176-206.

3. Austin, Granville, (1966). *The Indian Constitution Cornerstone of a Nation* (Oxford : Clarendon Press).

4. Bagchi, A., J.L. Bajaj, William A., Byrd (Eds.) (1992). *State Finances in India* (New Delhi : Vikas Publishing House Pvt. Ltd.).

5. Bajaj, J.L., K.S. Sinha and O.P. Aggarwal, (1985), *Finance Commission and Backward States* (Lucknow : Print House).

6. Bakhru, Mira, (1988). *Dynamics of Federal Bargaining*, (New Delhi : Intellectual Publishing House).

7. Banerjee, Anil Chandra, (1977-78). *The Constitutional History of India* : 1919 – 1977, Vol. III, (Delhi : Macmillan).

8. Basu, D.D., (1992). *Introduction to the Constitution of India* (Delhi : Prentice Hall of India).

9. Bhargava, Madhuri (1976). *Inter-Governmental Financial Relations in India since Independence* (Allahabad Chaitanya Publishing, House).

10. Bhargava, P.K. (1982). *Centre-State Resource Transfer in India* (Gurgaon: Academic Press).

11. Bhatnagar, Sudha, (1979). *Union – State Financial Relations and Finance Commissions* (Allahabad : Chugh Publications).

12. Bombwall, K.R., (1967). *The Foundation of Indian Federatism* (Delhi : Asia Publishing House).

13. *Ibid.*, (1977). *National Power and State Autonomy* (Meerut : Meenakshi Prakashan).

14. Bose, T.C., (1987). *Indian Federalism : Problems and Issues* (Calcutta : K.P. Bagchi).

15. Brass, Paul R., (1984). *Caste Faction and Party in Indian Politics*, Vol. I, (Delhi : Chanakya).

16. *Ibid.*, (1966). *Factional Politics in an Indian State : The Congress Party in U.P.* (Bombay : Oxford Press).

17. *Ibid.*, (1975). *Language, Religion and Politics in North India* (Delhi : Vikas Publishing House Pvt. Ltd.,).

18. Browne, E. and Franklin, M. (1973). 'Aspects of coalition payoffs in European parliamentary democracies', *American Political Science Review*, 67: 453-64.

19. Browne, E., Ferneries, J. and Gleiber, D. (1984). 'An events approach to the problem, cabinet stability', *Comparative Political Studies*, 17(2):167-97.

20. Bueno de Mesquita, B. (1975). Strategy, *Risk and personality in Coalition Politics: The Case of India,* Cambridge : Cambridge University Press.

21. Chabra, Harinder, K., (1977). *State Politics in India : Study of Centre-State Relations* (Delhi : Surjeet Publications.

22. Chakraborty, Bidyut (ed.) (1990). *Centre-State Relations in India* (Delhi : Segment Book Distributors).

23. Chand, Phul, (ed.) (1974). *Federal Financial Relations in India* (New Delhi: The Institute of Constitutional and Parliamentary Studies).

24. Chanda, Asok, (1965). *Federalism in India: A Study of Union – State Relations* (London : George Allen and Unwin).

25. Chandra, R.J., (1962). *Fiscal Policies in Underdeveloped Countries* (London : George Allen and Unwin).

26. Chandra Shekhar, S., (1988). *Indian Federalism and Autonomy* (Delhi : B.R. Publishing Corporation).

27. Chaturvedi, J.P. (1970). States of Our Union (Delhi : Government of India, Ministry of Information and Broadcasting, Publication Division).

28. Cook, T. (2002). *Nested Political Coalitions; Nation, Regime, Programe, Cabinet*, London: Praeger.

29. Coondoo, R., (196). *The Division of Powers in the Indian Constitution* (Calcutta : Book Land).

30. Dahiya, M.S., (1979). *Office of the Governor in India Critical Commentary* (Delhi : Sundeep Prakashan).

31. Dar, R.K., (1981). *Recent Development in Federal Financial Relations in India*, (Canberra : Centre for Federal Financial Relations, ANU).

32. Desai, A.R., (1973). *Recent Trends in Indian Nationalism* (Bombay : Popular Prakashan).

33. De Swaan, A. (1973). *Coalition Theories and Cabinet Formations*: A Study of Formal Theories of Coalition Formation Applied to Nine European Parliaments After 1918, London : Elsevier.

34. Dodd, I. (1976). *My South Block Years: Memoirs of a Foreign Secretary*, New Delhi: UBPSD.

35. Diwan, Paras, (1981). *Union-State Fiscal Relations : An Overview* (New Delhi : Light and Life Publishers).

36. Dua, B.D. and M.P. Singh (eds.) *Indian Federalism in the New Millennium*, New Delhi, Manohar, 2003.

37. Duverger, M. (1963). *Political Parties: Their Organization and Activity in the Modern State*, New York: Wiley.

38. Echeverri-Gent, J. (2002). 'Politics in India's decentred polity', in A. Ayres and P. Oldenburg (eds) *Indian Briefing: Quickening the Pace of Change*, New York: East Gate Book: 1953.

39. Eldersveld, S.J. (1971). *Political Parties : A Behavioural Analysis*, (Bombay : Vora and Company Publishers).

40. Euebbert, G. (1986). *Comparative Democracy: Policymaking and Governing Coalitions in Europe and Israel,* New York: Columbia University Press.

41. Fie, Victor, M., (1970). *Kerala : Yenan of India,* (Bombay : Nachiketa Publications Ltd.).

42. Financial Times (2003). 'BJP gains raise chances of early elections', Financial Times, 4 December.

43. Financial Times (2004b). 'Victorious BJP restarts reform drive in India', Financial Times, 6 December.

44. Frankel, Francine R., and Zoya Hasan (eds.). *Transforming India : Social and Political Dynamics of Democracy*, New Delhi, Oxford University Press, 2005.

45. Gadgil, D.R., (1947). *The Federal Problem of India* (Poona : Gokhle Institute of Politics and Economics).

46. Gehlot, N.S., (1977). *The Indian Office of the Governor – its Constitutional Image and Reality* (Allahabad : Chugh Publications).

47. George K.K., (1988). *Centre-State Financial Flows and Interstate Disparities* (Delhi : Criterion Books).

48. Graham, B.D. (1990). *Hindu Nationalism and Indian Politics: The Origins and Development of the Bharatiya Jana Sangh*, Cambridge: Cambridge University Press.

49. Grewal, B.S., (1974). *Fiscal Federalism in India* (Canberra : Centre for Research on Federal Financial Relations. The Australian National University.

50. Ghosh, B.N., (1985). *Political Economy of Neocolonialism in Third World Countries*, (Delhi : Sterling Publishers Pvt. Ltd.).

51. Gopa Kumar G., (1984). *The Congress Party and State Politics* (New Delhi: Deep and Deep Publications).

52. Gopalan, A.K., (1959). *Kerala : Past and Present* (London : Lawrence and Wishart).

53. Govindan Nair, M.N., (1957). *Challenge of Kerala* (Delhi).

54. Gupta, U.N. (ed.) (1988). *Indian Federalism and Unity of Nation : A Review of Indian Constitutional Experience* (Allahabad: Vohra Publishers).

55. Haksar, K.M., and Panikkar, K.M., (1930). *Federal India* (London : Martin Hopkinson).

56. Hansen, T. (1999). *The Saffron Wave: Democracy and Hindu Nationalism in Modern India*, Princeton: Princeton University Press.

57. Hansen, T. and Jaffrelot, C. (eds) (1998a). *The BJP and the Compulsions of Politics in India*, Delhi: Oxford University Press.

58. Hansen, T. and Jaffrelot, C. (1998b). 'Introduction: The BJP after the 1996 elections', in T. Hasen and C. Jaffrelot (eds) *The BJP and the Compulsions of Politics in India*, Delhi : Oxford University Press : pp. 1-21.

59. Hardgrave, R. and Kochanek, S. (1993). *India: Government and Politics in a Developing Nation*, 5th edn, London: Harcourt Brace College Publishers.

60. Haqqi, S.A.H. (ed.) (1967) : *Union-State Relations in India*, (Meerut, Meenakshi Prakashan).

61 *Ibid.*, (ed.) (1984). *Democracy, Pluralism and Nation-Building*, (Delhi : N.B.O).

62. Hardgrave, R.L. (Jr.) (1979). *Essays in the Political Sociology of South India* (New Delhi : Usha Publications).

63. Hartmann, Horst, (1971). *Political Parties in India* (Meerut : Meenakshi Prakashan).

64. Hussain, M.A. (1989). *Socio-Legal Perspective of Centre-State Relations in India* (New Delhi : Deep and Deep Publications).

65. India Today (2002b). 'Politics of trust', India Today, 13 August: 20-1.

66. Jaffrelot, C. (1996). *The Hindu Nationalist Movement and Indian Politics, 1925 to the 1990s; Strategies of Identity-Building Implantation and Mobilization (with Special Reference to Central India),* London: Hurst and Company.

67. Jaffrelot, C. (2000). 'Hindu nationalism and democracy', in F. Frankel (ed.) *Transforming India: Social and Political Dynamics of Democracy*, Delhi and Oxford: Oxford University Press: pp. 353-78.

68. Jain, R.B., (1976). *The Indian Parliament : Innovations, Reform and Development* (Calcutta : Minerva Associates).

69. Jain, S.N. and Other (eds.) (1972). *The Union and the States* (Delhi : National).

70. Jennings, Sir Ivor (1953). *Some Characteristics of the Indian Constitution* (London : Oxford University Press).

71. Jenkins, R. (2003a). *'How federalism influences India's domestic politics of WTO engagement (an is itself affected in the process)*', Asian Survey, 43(4): pp. 598-621.

72. John P. John, (1983). *Coalition Government in Kerala* (Trivandrum : Institute for the Study of Public Policy and Management).

73. Johari, J.C. (1977). *Indian Government and Politics* (Delhi : Vishal).

74. Jose Chander, N., (1981). *The Legislative Process in Kerala* (Trivandrum).

75. *Ibid.*, (1986). *Dynamics of State Politics : Kerala* (Delhi : Sterling Publishers Pvt. Ltd.).

76. Katju, M. (2003) *Vishwa Hindu Parishad and India Politics*, Hyderabad: Orient Longman.

77. Kashypa, Subhash C., (ed.) (1972). *Indian Parties and Politics* (New Delhi: Institute of Constitutional and Parliamentary Studies).

78. *Ibid.*, (ed.) (1969). *Union-State Relations in India* (New Delhi: Institute of Constitutional and Parliamentary Studies).

79. *Ibid.*, (1971). *Indian Political Parties* (Delhi : Research).

80. Khan, Shafa'at Ahmad (1937). *Indian Federation : An Exposition and Critical Review* (London).

81. Khan, Rasheeduddin (1994). *Bewildered India : Identity, Pluralism, Discord*, New Delhi : Har Anand Publications.

82. Kochanek, S.A. (1968). *The Congress Party of India : The Dynamics of One Party Democracy*, (Princeton : New Jersey).

83. Koshy, M.J. (1972). *Genesis of Political Consciousness in Kerala* (Trivandrum : Kerala Historical Society).

84. Kothari, Rajni (ed.) (1967). *Party, System and Election Studies* (Bombay : Allied Publishers).

85. *Ibid.*, (1972). *Politics in India* (Bombay : Orient Longman).

86. *Ibid.*, (1989). *Politics and the People : In Search of Humane India*, (Vol. I and II, New Delhi : Ajanta Publications).

87. *Ibid.*, (1988). *State Against Democracy : In Search of Humane Governance* (New Delhi : Ajanta Publications).

88. Krishnamurthy, K.G. and Lakshmana Rao, G., (1968). *Political Preferences in Kerala : An Electoral Analysis of Kerala General Elections, 1957, 1960 and 1967* (New Delhi : Radha Krishna Prakashan).

89. Krishnaswami, A., (1965). *The Indian Union and the States : A Study in Anatomy and Integration*, (London : Pergamon Press).

90. Kumar Pradeep, (1988). *Studies in Indian Federalism*, (New Delhi : Deep and Deep Publications).

91. Lakdawala, D.T., (1967). *Union-State Financial Relations* (Bombay : Lawani Publishing House).

92. Lal, Mukut Behari, (1958). *Indicatment of U.P. Government Praja Socialist Party* (Lucknow : Sardar Press).

93. Livingston, W.S., (1956). *Federalism and the Constitutional Change,* (Oxford : Clarendon Press).

94. Laver, M. and Budge, (eds) (1992). *Party Policy and Government Coalitions,* New York; St Martin's Press.

95. Laver, M and Schofield, N. (1990). *Multiparty Government: The Politics of Coalition in Europe*, Oxford: Oxford University Press.

96. Linz, Stepan, A. and Yadav, Y. (2004). 'Nation State' or 'State Nation'? *'Comparative reflections on Indian democracy'*, paper presented at the third NET-SAPPE meeting in Paris, 28-30 June.

97. Livingston, W.S., (1956). *Federalism and the Constitutional Change,* (Oxford : Clarendon Press).

98. Maheshwari, B.L., (ed.) (1973). *Centre-State Relations in the Seventies* (Calcutta : Minerva Associates).

99. Maheshwari, B.L. (ed.) (1977). *Presidents' Rule in India* (New Delhi : Macmillan).

100. *Ibid.*, (1979). *State Government in India* (New Delhi : Macmillan).

101. *Ibid.*, (1981). *Indian Parliamentary System* (Agra : Lakshmi Narain Aggarwal).

102. Majeed, Akhtar (ed.) (1984). *Regionalism : Development Tensions in India*. (New Delhi : Cosmo Publications).

103. Manor, J. (1995). 'Regional parties in federal systems', in D. Verney and B. Arora (eds) *Multiple Identities in a Single State: Indian Federalism in Comparative Perspective*, Delhi: Konark Publishers: pp. 105-35.

104. Manor, J. (1996). *'Ethnicity and politics in India'*, *International Affairs*, 72(1): pp. 459-75.

105. Manor, J. (1998) 'Southern discomfort: The BJP in Karnataka', in T. Hansen and C. Jaffrelot (eds). *The BJP and the Compulsion of Politics in India,* Delhi: Oxford University Press : pp. 163-201.

106. Manor, J. (2000). 'Small-time political fixers in Indian states: '*Towel over armpit*', *Asian Survey* (September – October): pp. 816-35.

107. Manor, J. (2001). 'Centre-state relations', in A. Kohli, *The Success of India's Democracy,* Cambridge: Cambridge University Press : pp. 78-102.

108. Mathur, P.L., (1988). *Role of Governor in Non-Congress States,* Jaipur : Rawat Publications.

109. Mawdsley, E. (2002). '*Redrawing the body politics: federalism*', *regionalism and the creation of new states in India*', Commonwealth and Comparative Politics, 40(s); pp. 34-54.

110. Mershon, C. (2002). *The Costs of Coalitions, Stanford,* California: Stanford University Press.

111. Mitra, Subrata Kumar, (1978). *Governmental Instability in Indian States* (Ajanta Publications, Delhi).

112. Mogi, Sobei, (1931). *The Problem of Federalism,* Vol. I, (London : George Allen and Unwin).

113. Morris – Jones, W.H., (1974). *Government and Politics in India* (New Delhi : B.I. Publications).

114. *Ibid.*, (1978). *Politics Mainly Indian* (Bombay : Orient Longman).

115. Mukharjee, A.B., (1967). *Parliamentary Procedure in India* (Calcutta : O.U.P).

116. Namboodiripad, E.M.S., (1968). 2nd edn. *Kerala : Yesterday, Today and Tomorrow* (Calcutta : National Book Agency).

117. Narain, Iqbal (ed.) (1976). *State Politics in India* (Meerut : Meenakshi Prakashan).

118. Noorani, A.G., (ed.) (1972). *Centre-State Relations in India* (Bombay : Orient House).

119. Nossiter, T.J., (1982). *Communism in Kerala* (Delhi : Oxford University Press).

119. Pal, Chandra (1983). *Centre-State Relations and Cooperative Federalism* (New Delhi : Deep and Deep Publications).

120. Palmer, Norman D., (1971). *The Indian Political System* (Boston : Houghton Mifflin Co.).

121. *Ibid.*, (1976). *Elections and Political Development* (New Delhi: Vikas Publishing House).

122. Pandey, Jawahar Lal, (1982). *State Politics in India* (New Delhi : Uppal Publishing House).

123. Panvar, R.D., (1980). *Economic Federation* (Delhi : Pragati Publications).

124. Park, Richard L., and Tinker, Irene (ed.) (1960). *Leadership and Political Institutions in India* (Madras : Oxford University Press).

125. Patil, S. (2001). *'India's experiment with coalition government at the federal level'*, Indian Journal of Political Science, 62(4): pp. 586-93.

126. Prakash, Karat, (1973). *Language and Nationality Politics in India* (Bombay : Orient Longman).

127. Prasad, Anirudh (1981). *Presidential Government or Parliamentary Democracy* (New Delhi : Deep and Deep Publications).

128. *Ibid.*, (1985). *Centre-State Relations in India : Constitutional Provisions, Judicial Reviews, Recent Trends* (New Delhi : Deep and Deep Publications).

129. Powell, G. (1981). 'Party systems and political system performance: Voting participation, government stability and mass violence in contemporary democracies', *American Political Science Review,* 75(4): pp. 861-79.

130. Pridham, G. (ed.) (1986). Coalitional Behaviour in Theory and Practice: An Inductive Model for Western Europe, Cambridge: Cambridge University Press.

131. Pye, Lucian W., and Verba Sidney (ed.) (1965). *Political Culture and Political Development* (New Jersey : Princeton).

132. Pylee, M.V., (1977). *Constitutional Government in India* (Bombay : Asia Publishing House).

133. Rajendran, G., (1974). *The Ezhava Community and Kerala Politics* (Trivandrum : Kerala Academy of Political Science).

134. Ramakrishnan Nair, (1964). *Constitutional Experiments in Kerala* (Trivandrum : Kerala Academy of Political Science).

135. *Ibid.*, (1965). How Communists Came to Power in Kerala (Trivandrum : Kerala Academy of Political Science).

136. Ram, D. and Gehlot, N. (2000). 'Coalition politics in India (search for political stability)', *Indian Journal of Public Administration*, XLVI (4): pp. 733-5.

137. Raman, V. (2001). *'The women's question in contemporary Indian politics'*, Asian Journal of Women's Studies, 7(2): pp. 39-71.

138. Rao, K.V., (1961). *Parliamentary Democracy of India* (Calcutta : The World Press Pvt. Ltd.)

139. Rao, N.R., (1972). *Union-State Financial Relations in India* (Karnataka University, Dharwar).

140. Rath, Sharda, (1984). *Federalism Today* (New Delhi : Sterling Publishers).

141. Ravindran, T.K., (1978). *Institutions and Movements in Kerala History* (Trivandrum).

142. Ray, Amal, (1979). *Federal Politics and Government* (New Delhi : The Macmillan Company of India Ltd.).

143. *Ibid.*, (1966). *Inter Governmental Relations in India* (Bombay: Asia Publishing House.

144. *Ibid.*, (1970). *Tension Areas in India's Federal System* (Calcutta : World Press).

145. Ray, Bharati, (1967). *Evolution of Federalism in India* (Calcutta : Progressive Publishers).

146. Reagon, Michael D., (1972). *The New Federalism* (New York: Oxford Press).

147. Riker, W. (1962). *The Theory of Political Coalitions*, New Haven: Yale University Press. Riker, W and Ordeshook. P. (1973) *An Introduction to Positive Political Theory*, Englewood Clefts: Prentice Hall.

148. Riker, William, H., (1964). *Federalism* (Boston : Little Brown).

149. Rosen, Georgc, (1966). *Democracy and Economic Change in India* (Bombay : Vora and Co. Publishers Pvt. Ltd.).

150. Roy, N.C. (1962). *Federalism and the Linguistic States* (Calcutta : Firma K.L. Mukhopadhyay).

151. Roy, Ramashray, (1973). *Uncertain Verdict : A Study of the 1969 Elections in Four States* (New Delhi : Orient Longman).

152. Sadasivan, Nair, Dr. K., (1984). *Congress and Kerala Politics* (Trivandrum).

153. Saez Lawrence, *Federalism Without a Centre*, New Delhi, Sage Publication, 2002.

154. Sahni, N.C. (ed.) (1971). *Coalition Politics in India* (Jullunder: New Academic Publishing House).

155. Sahni, Sati, (ed.) (1984). *Centre-State Relations* (New Delhi: Vikas Publishing House).

155. Sampurnanand, (1962). *Memories and Reflections* (Bombay: Asia Publishing House).

156. Santhanam, K. (1960). *Union-State Relations in India* (Bombay : Asia Publishing House).

157. Sastry, M.L. and Reddy, G.R., (1988). *Centre-State of Financial Relations: A Study in Levels of Development of States* (New Delhi : Concept Publications).

158. Saxena, K.S., (1985). *Indian Democracy : Recent Trends and Issues* (New Delhi : Anmol Publications).

159. Sen, Ashok K., (1975). *Role of Governor in the Emerging Pattern of Centre State Relations in India* (New Delhi : National).

160. Shankhdher, M.M., (ed.) (1983). *Framework of Indian Politics* (New Delhi : Gitanjali).

161. Sharma, P.K., (1969). *Political Aspects of States Reorganisation in India* (New Delhi : Mohini Publications).

162. Sharma, T.R., (ed.) (1986). *New Challenges of Politics in Indian States* (New Delhi : Uppal Publications).

163. Singh, G. (1997a) .'The Coalition Experience', *Indian Journal of Political Science*, LVIII (1-4): pp. 39-54.

164. Singh, M.P. (2001). *'India's National Front and United Front coalition governments*: a phase in federalised governance', Asian Survey, XLI (2): pp. 328-50.

165. Singhvi, L.M., (ed.) (1972). *Parliament and Administration in India* (New Delhi : Institute of Constitutional and Parliamentary Studies).

166. Siwach, J.R., (1977). *The Office of Governor : A Critical Analysis – 1950-73* (New Delhi : Sterling Publishers).

167. Spann, R.N., (ed).) (1963). *Constitutionalism in India* (Bombay : Asia Publishing House).

168. Spratt, P. (1970). *D.M.K. in Power* (Bombay : Nachiketa Publications).

169. Sridharan, E. (2002). 'The fragmentation of the Indian party system, 1952-1999: seven competing explanations', in Z. Hasan (ed.) *Parties and Party Politics in India*, Oxford: Oxford University Press: pp. 475-503.

170. Srivastava, Meera, (1980). *Constitutional Crisis in the States in India,* (New Delhi : Concept Publishing Co.).

171. Subba Rao, K. (1972). *The Indian Federal System* (Madras : Institute for Techno-Economic Studies).

172. Sukumaran Nayar, Dr. V.K., (ed.) (1969). *Kerala Society and Politics* (Trivandrum).

173. Suresh, C.P., (1983). *Political Behaviour in Kerala* (Trivandrum : Institute for the Study of Policy and Management).

174. Suryamurthy, R. (2003). *'NDA allies may forum to 'Check' BJP'*, The Tribune, 3 October, Online, Available at http:// www.tribuncindia.com /2003/20031003/ national.htm (accessed 9 February 2004).

175. Thimmaiah, G., (1985). *Burning Issues in Centre-State Financial Relations* (New Delhi : Ashish Publishing House).

176. Tiwari, Umakant, (1967). *The Making of the Indian Constitution* (Allahabad: Central Book Depot).

177. Tripathy, R.N. (1982). *Federal Finance and Economic Development in India* (New Delhi : Sterling Publishers).

178. Vajpayee, A. (1998). 'Statement to the Lok Sabha, 27th May 1998'. Online, Available at: http://www.indiatoday.com/ ntoday/cabinet.html (accessed 28 May 1998).

179. Varshney, A. and Sridharan, E. (2001). 'Towards moderate pluralism: political parties in India', in L. Diamond and R. Gunther (eds.) *Political Parties and Democry*, Baltimore: Johns Hopkins University Press: 207-37.

180. Veeravaghavachar, S.M., (1969). *Union-State Financial Relations* (New Delhi : Sterling Publishers).

181. Venkatarangaiya, M. and Shiviah M., (1975). *Indian Federalism* (New Delhi : Arnold – Hinemann).

182. Verma, Ganeshi Lal (1978). *Party Politics in U.P.* (Delhi : Sandeep).

183. Verma, S.L., (1987). *Federal Authority in the Indian Political System* (Jaipur : R.B.S.A. Publishers).

184. Wallace, Paul (ed.) (1985). *Region and Nation in India* (New Delhi : American Institute).

185. Weiner, Myron (1957). *Party Politics in India : The Development of a Multiparty System* (New Jersy : Princeton).

186. *Ibid.*, (1963). *Political Change in South Asia* (Calcutta : Firama K.L. Mukhopadhyaya).

187. *Ibid.*, (1963). *The Politics of Scarcity* (Bombay: Asia Publishing House).

188. *Ibid.*, (ed.) (1968). *State Politics in India* (Princeton : Princeton University Press).

189. Wright, T. (2001). '*The impact of coalition politics in India on Indian minorities*: the case of Muslims and Christians', Indian Journal of Secularism, 5(2) July/September: pp. 1-7.

190. Wyatt, A. (1999), 'The limitations on coalition politics in India: the case of electoral alliances in Uttar Pradesh', *Commonwealth and Comparative Politics*, 37(2): pp. 1-21.

Index